MORE THAN PETTICOATS

Remarkable
KANSAS WOMEN

MORE THAN PETTICOATS

Remarkable KANSAS WOMEN

Gina Kaufmann

Guilford, Connecticut

To buy books in quantity for corporate use
or incentives, call **(800) 962-0973**
or e-mail **premiums@GlobePequot.com.**

Map by Daniel Lloyd © Morris Book Publishing, LLC
Project editor: Meredith Dias
Layout: Sue Murray

Library of Congress Cataloging-in-Publication Data
Kaufmann, Gina.
  More than petticoats. Remarkable Kansas women / Gina Kaufmann.
    p. cm.
  Includes bibliographical references and index.
  ISBN 978-0-7627-6027-5
  1. Women—Kansas—Biography. 2. Women—Kansas—History. 3.
Kansas—Biography. I. Title. II. Title: Remarkable Kansas women.
  CT3262.K36K38 2012
  920.078—dc23

                                                    2011038664
Printed in the United States of America
10 9 8 7 6 5 4 3 2 1

CONTENTS

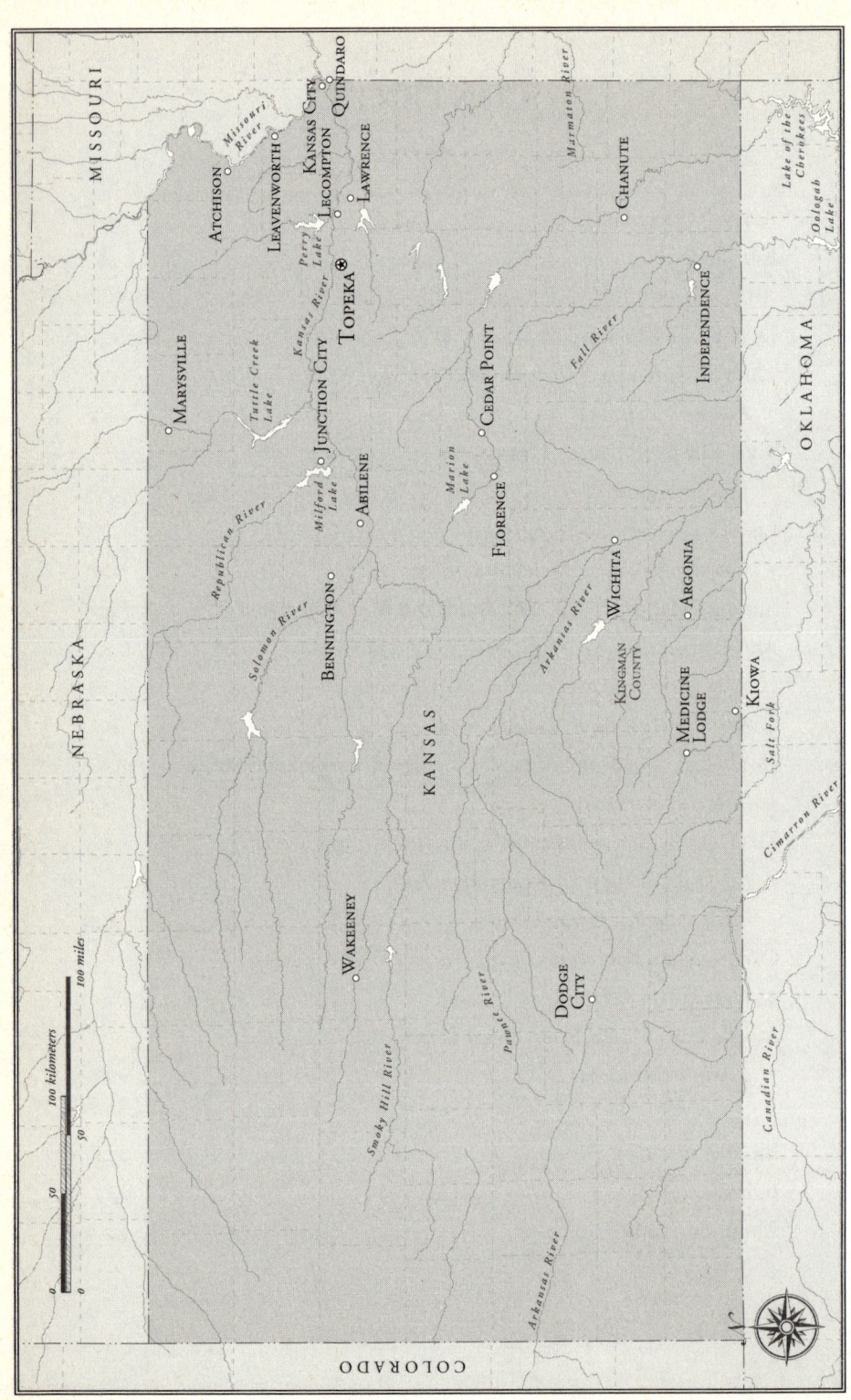

ACKNOWLEDGMENTS

I enjoyed getting to know these women over the course of the last year. I met more of them than I was able to include in these pages. That is why the first people I would like to acknowledge are the women I did not include, because they also amazed and inspired me.

I would like to acknowledge the good people at the research institutions that helped me along the way: the Kansas City Public Library, the Kansas State Historical Society, Haskell Indian Nations University Cultural Center & Museum, the Safari Museum, the Harvey House Museum, and the Kenneth Spencer Research Library at the University of Kansas.

Thanks to my many families for supporting me in countless ways. To all the Kaufmanns, Padorrs, Spitcaufskys, Baums, Loebs, and Smiths out there: I love you.

A special thank you to fellow Kansas writer Sarah Smarsh, for being my colleague no matter where we work, and to Alex Smith, whose kindness makes everything easier, and whose discipline, creativity, and intellect remind me to expect much of myself.

I dedicate this book to my Aunt Camille—or, as my dad used to call her, the Boss. She passed away as I began working on this book. I don't know where she is now, but I hope everyone there is following her orders. Rest in peace, Boss. This one's for you.

INTRODUCTION

—◦•◦—

"'I Been Working on the Railroad.' There's just two things I'm worried about with that: the grammar and the use of slave labor."
—Lorrie Moore

This pithy little one-liner, from Lorrie Moore's novel *A Gate at the Stairs,* comes close to summarizing the sentiments likely to wash over a modern-day reader discovering the lives of nineteenth-century Kansans.

Let's review the items in order: railroad, grammar, slavery.

The story of nineteenth-century Kansas is, in large part, a story of railroads. The railroads shaped the land. They populated it. They gave people jobs, in many cases, or took those jobs away in other cases. They influenced political decisions that influenced lives. They built lives, and they ruined lives. Or else they were just blamed for ruining lives. It's a tough call to make. But the story of the railroad is at the heart of almost every single story in this book.

At the heart, but not the heart itself. The heart of each story is the heart of a woman who did something brave, unexpected, difficult, or inspired. Usually all of the above.

Next, grammar. Almost all of these women were teachers for some period of time. Dentist Lucy Hobbs Taylor started as a teacher. Classical music composer Nora Holt also spent some time as a teacher. So did a leader of the Kansas Populist movement, Mary Lease. The list goes on— one need only consult the contents. I did not directly profile any teachers for the simple reason that, indirectly, almost every profile describes a teacher. But I would be remiss in not mentioning that in the nineteenth century, the women of Kansas formed a stalwart teaching army: courageous, hard-working, and severely underpaid. And just because it was a field that welcomed women with open arms does not render the work done by teachers any less important than the work done in other fields.

The language in this book may occasionally get folksy between quotation marks. But more striking is the brilliant wordsmithery these women almost unanimously exhibit. I hope their clever turns of phrase serve to unravel unflattering stereotypes of rural middle-of-the-mappers. I am proud to call these women my geographical ancestors.

Finally, slave labor. This is perhaps the stickiest issue of all. Kansas takes great pride in its Civil War–era status as a Free State. The Kansas-Missouri border was a dramatic place to be in the nineteenth century, as it was not just the border between states but also the border between North and South.

One of the stories is about an escaped slave seeking freedom along the Underground Railroad. Readers from Kansas might be startled to learn that Ann Clarke was not a Missouri slave seeking freedom in Kansas. She was, in fact, a Kansas slave. This information might be upsetting; I know it upset me. Kansas was admitted as a free state in 1861, but territories—not being states—were settled without definitive rules governing such things. When Kansas was still a mere territory, a handful of slave owners did settle there. Now, they were not numerous, and their neighbors—predisposed toward freedom—did not make life easy for them. But they existed.

For those Free Staters who have been raised to take pride in their state's non-slaveholding past, this will be an understandably tough pill to swallow. So I am preparing you now, hopefully allowing you to read Ann's story with an appreciation of her bravery—as opposed to pure, unmitigated disappointment. Though a little disappointment is certainly merited.

In a few stories, racially sensitive hindsight might make modern-day readers uncomfortable. I mention this not to excuse the subjects profiled for words or actions that make us squeamish, but to say in advance that I, too, recoiled at times. All I can offer is my belief that the characters profiled in this book were ahead of their time, even if by today's standards they admittedly fall short.

LUCY HOBBS TAYLOR

(1833–1910)
THE WOMAN WHO PULLED TEETH

Pulling teeth is a famously excruciating experience. It is so universally dreaded and reviled that anything else that is dreaded and reviled is said to be "like pulling teeth." Yet for the dentist, pulling teeth is just another day at the office. And for the aspiring dentist, pulling teeth is but a dream.

That was the case for Lucy Hobbs.

Lucy was born in 1833 in upstate New York, in a community where roads had been laid just prior to her birth. She was one of ten children raised in a log cabin on Yankee pluck, as she called it, and little else. She was only ten years old when she lost her mother, and she was orphaned by the age of twelve. She and her siblings had to fend for themselves, relying heavily on the oldest sister, Hannah, until they were able to scrape by on their own. Lucy took work as a seamstress from a very young age to pitch in. But still, in spite of her troubles at home, she rarely missed a day of school. When she was sixteen, Lucy went into teaching—a career she knew she could count on to support herself. She landed a job in Brooklyn, Michigan, a mill town like the town where she grew up in New York State, surrounded by the dense wilderness of the Great Lakes region.

Lucy was fascinated with medicine, science, and the human body, and she studied these subjects on the side with a local physician. She didn't dare pursue her interest in medicine beyond casual study until she had built up the confidence and resources she would need to make the leap with assurance. A medical education would cost a pretty penny, and she would have to earn it first. Furthermore, attempting to become a physician would require her to put her reputation as a woman on the

1

Lucy Hobbs Taylor Kansas Historical Society

line. The move could affect her social standing, possibly to the point of jeopardizing the career she already had as a teacher.

To get a sense of the accepted views on women entering the medical field, let us consult a resolution on the subject, drafted by Harvard University students in 1850:

Resolved, That no woman of true delicacy would be willing in the presence of men to listen to the discussions of subjects that necessarily come under the consideration of the student of medicine.

There was a handful of women so interested in medicine that public scorn and constant questioning of their femininity did not dissuade them. These hardy ladies often moved out to the western territories, where doctors were so few and dangers to one's health so abundant that the odds seemed to work in their favor. Eventually, they thought, patients would become desperate enough for medical attention that they would set aside their misgivings and allow themselves to be treated by a female physician. But even those women who worked as doctors in the territories were discouraged from going out at night or making house calls; it was believed that going out alone would make them vulnerable to attacks from those who found their career choice offensive. The very few who did go out risked their lives to do so and often disguised themselves in men's clothing for a little extra protection.

To say that women in medicine in nineteenth-century America were forced to endure a hostile work environment would be putting it mildly.

Most medical schools explicitly refused to so much as consider female applicants for admission. The one exception, in 1859, was the Eclectic College of Medicine in Cincinnati, Ohio. At the urging of her tutor, Lucy moved to Cincinnati to apply.

A few months before the application was due, the Eclectic College of Medicine added a statute much like those already in place at other medical schools barring the admission of women. But one of the instructors there—seeing Lucy's determination, and being in some ways magnetically drawn to controversy—took her under his wing, offering to continue her private studies of medicine where she had left off back in Michigan. She rented out a tiny attic apartment, and spent her nights doing seamstress work by candlelight to eke out a living.

One day, while helping Lucy with her studies, her mentor made the casual observation that dentistry might be more open to women than general medicine, adding that the dentist doesn't have to make house calls or go trudging through town in awful weather or at night. The patient comes to the dentist, not the other way around. From his perspective, this would make dentistry quite appealing.

Dentistry was the "wild west" of medicine: It was a field almost entirely lacking in rules or regulations of any kind. The pulling of teeth, in fact, was not much more than a sideshow act. The profession had not moved far beyond the days when itinerant actor-dentists, barber-dentists, and wig maker–dentists set up shop under tents and shaved beards, trimmed hair, put on plays, and treated toothaches. Dental schools existed, and they were smiled upon but not viewed as necessary to the training of a dentist. It was entirely possible and not the least bit uncommon for uncertified dentists to set up shop and treat patients. They learned the trade by apprenticeship, as though they were cobblers or bakers, except that instead of banging on shoe soles or kneading dough, they were reaching into people's mouths with pliers. Even people inclined toward nostalgia and romanticizing the past have to acknowledge that when it comes to dentistry, we are fortunate to have left the nineteenth century behind.

But Lucy's mentor's passing observations about dentistry piqued her interest nonetheless. She wanted a career where she could support herself handsomely with a job that matched her intellect. She did not want to toil sewing hems on clothes for a pittance for the rest of her life when she knew she had what it took to do the things smart men did: things that paid better and did not hurt their hands.

Prospective dental students in the nineteenth century completed apprenticeships before applying to dental school, so Lucy's first step was to seek out a local dentist under whom she could study as an apprentice. She approached dentist after dentist and had two basic conversation templates, with details varying only slightly. There was the conversation in which the dentist berated her for forgetting that her place was in the home, not the office. "But they forgot," she later wrote, "nay worse, some of them did not care, that I had no home—and that was the main reason I wanted to learn dentistry." And then there was the conversation in which the dentist informed her that he would love to give her an apprenticeship, but that threatened to ruin his reputation and cost him needed patients.

One dentist offered the following compromise: Lucy could work for him as a maid, cleaning his office and examining room, observing, and learning furtively out of the corner of her eye while she swept and scrubbed. This arrangement would suit him just fine, he added, so long as she did not let anyone know she was learning from him. She would have to keep up the Cinderella charade. Lucy had just enough pride to indignantly refuse his offer. She kept looking for an apprenticeship and kept being turned away.

It took superhuman perseverance to keep knocking on doors in the face of repeated rejection. But her determination eventually paid off when she knocked on the door of a man whose name is spelled differently almost everywhere it is written. Maybe his name was Dr. Samuel Wardell. Maybe his name was Dr. Samuel Wardle. But whatever his name was, Lucy Hobbs believed it should be hallowed. "To him alone belongs the honor of making it possible for women to enter the profession," she wrote. "He was to us what Queen Isabella was to Columbus."

She continued to study during the day and sew in her attic at night in order to earn a few pennies for a morning meal. Her previous, intense study of medical concepts made her a proficient student of dentistry who advanced quickly. Within three months, she was making artificial porcelain teeth—now called dentures—on her own.

This set of porcelain teeth was submitted to the Ohio Mechanics Institute's Eighteenth Exhibition, where it won a medal for showing "a marked degree of superiority over the others."

But now, it was time to apply to dental school. In 1861, she submitted her application to the Ohio College of Dental Surgery, the foremost school of dentistry. She was not the only unconventional applicant that year. The school also received an application from a man who had been born in Liberia in West Africa. A faculty meeting was called to discuss these applicants: the woman and the African. Staff members engaged in lively discussion and then held a vote: By a vote of four to two, the applicants were denied admission to dental school. The school went so far as to pass a resolution that neither women nor people of African descent would be admitted to the Ohio College of Dental Surgery.

Dr. Wardell, or Wardle—good ol' what's-his-name—was convinced that his star pupil did not need a dental certificate to open up a successful dental practice. At the time, very few of his male colleagues had diplomas hanging on their walls. Lucy could simply do as they had done: open a practice and learn from experience. She had completed her apprenticeship and proven her knowledge and ability. She had worked with patients. There was no reason to let rejection from dental schools stop her.

She followed her mentor's advice and opened a practice in Cincinnati. Things got off to a rough start. She earned a quarter per tooth pulled, and often had only a quarter to her name at the end of a slow week. Cincinnati had plenty of other established dentists, and it would take some time for her to make a name for herself, or at least to become known as something more than a novelty.

And then the Civil War broke out. Lucy received word that four of her brothers had joined Union forces back home in New York. In Ohio, a border state, business came to a standstill. Men left to fight, and fatherless families struggled to make ends meet. Violence raged on the streets, and even those who could afford dental services stayed home unless going out was a matter of life or death. Even well-established dentists and businesspeople of all kinds struggled to stay afloat in that languishing wartime economy.

Becoming ever more accustomed to her penchant for bad timing, Lucy did what she had always done: She counted her losses and moved on. A friend lent her money to travel to Iowa, where she settled and tried again, embarking on her second venture as a journeyman dentist.

In Iowa, the local Indians referred to her as "the woman who pulls teeth." Here, the novelty of her gender worked in her favor, setting her apart from dentists and attracting customers whose curiosity simply could not be satisfied in any way except to have their own teeth pulled by this lady extractor.

By the end of her first year in business, she had one hundred dollars left over after expenses were paid. This was just enough to buy herself a dentist's chair, but it was a start. She went into her second year ready for business. She took her dentist's chair and moved to a better location—smack dab in the middle of the bustling town of McGregor, Iowa, where she expected more patients to come limping in agony through her office door, begging to have their aching teeth pulled. A dentist's dream come true.

She was right about her new location. She finished up her second year in business with three thousand dollars in the bank—a veritable fortune in 1862. Even more important than her favorable bank balance was her growing reputation. Everyone in Iowa knew that the "woman who pulls teeth" could be counted on to do quality work. In a sea of itinerant dentists, Lucy stood out. Her willingness to stand by a permanent, brick-and-mortar location told patients that she would remain accountable for her work instead of disappearing into the night before the pain returned the next day.

Due to increased respect from patients and colleagues alike, Lucy was invited to a meeting of the recently formed Iowa Dental Society, made up mostly of those rare creatures who had actual dental certification. She wasn't sure what to do. It was an honor to be invited—of course, she appreciated that—but closing her office would mean losing money and running the risk of losing patients to competitors. Reluctantly she decided to hang a sign in her windows, lock the the door behind her, and head to Dubuque for the conference.

She shook hands with the president of the society. She sat and listened to presentations on the newest innovations and debates regarding the use of certain tools for certain procedures. Finally, after listening for hours, Lucy was asked directly for her opinion on the use of the lancet in tooth-pulling procedures. Her answer was demure but confident. After explaining that she had come to listen and not to speak, she allowed that she found the lancet to be a valuable tool. Three-fourths of her business was tooth extraction, she explained, and in her experience, patients complained less of pain when she used the lancet than when she did not. Her colleagues listened attentively as she spoke, a confidence booster that was worth the financial sacrifice required for the trip all on its own. She would later describe the respect she received at the convention as a "balm for many old wounds."

The president of the association then stood up to make an announcement. He announced, before all who had gathered there, that the Iowa State Dental Society had elected to admit a "lady practitioner of dentistry" for membership in its ranks by unanimous vote. He was talking about Lucy Hobbs.

She thanked the society and expressed her determination to do good work in the profession so that they would never regret their decision. The Dental Society quickly heaped upon her one more honor: She should be sent as part of the state's delegation to a national dentists' meeting in Chicago. Little did she know that the other members of the Iowa delegation demanded that the Ohio College of Dental Surgery make up for its past wrongdoing in refusing to admit Lucy Hobbs as a student. If the Ohio school did not admit her, the delegation said, then the state of Iowa would secede from the national association on her behalf. Because most of the Ohio College of Dental Surgery's faculty was at the meeting, its members got together and voted once again on whether to admit Lucy Hobbs—now a thirty-two-year-old woman who had five years professional experience and a thriving business to her name, as well as the state of Iowa backing her up. The verdict was different this time around. Lucy was guaranteed admission, if only she would renew her application. So she applied, once again, to dental school. And this time, she was accepted. She would enroll as a senior, in acknowledgment of her extensive background in dentistry.

The only woman in a class of nineteen aspiring dentists, Lucy graduated at the top of her class. One of her professors stated that "her opinion was asked and her opinion sought in difficult cases almost daily by her fellow students." On February 21, 1866, she became the first woman to receive a copy of the Sacred Scriptures and the doctor of dental surgery degree (DDS). Following this event, an article belittling Lucy appeared in *The Dental Times*. A publication called *The Dental Register* offered a rebuttal, asking her detractor to have a tooth filled by Dr. Lucy. "Get her to fill a tooth for you (if you have no decayed ones, let her drill a hole in a sound one) and your objections to lady dentists will vanish into thin air. The doctor will do it well."

The public seconded the school's decision to open the profession's doors to women. An editorial writer for the *Cincinnati Dental Reporter* wrote, "Even now we almost imagine ourselves seated in what is usually termed the 'chair of torture'—dreaded now no more—by our side a beautiful lady, with sweet breath and glowing cheek, her delicate arm encircling our head. . . . With such a dentist, we would want our teeth examined every twenty-four hours."

This author was not the only one to get a bit carried away in his imaginings of the care he might receive from the lady dentist. Across the ocean, in England, a poem titled "To a Lady Dentist" was published in 1887. From the four-stanza poem come the following lines:

Welcome is the hand that comes
Lightly hovering o're my gums
Not a throne, love, could compare
To thine operating chair.
Lady dentist, fair to see
Are the forceps held by thee

But the story stays close to home. Lucy did not rest on her laurels. She got back to work. After receiving her diploma, the first place Lucy went to expand her practice was Chicago. There she fell in love with and swiftly married Civil War veteran James Taylor, who had fought against slavery and now worked for the railroads. He was an artist and a painter by passion, and suffered from wartime injuries never named with any precision, though the vague description of symptoms from which he did not recover sound a bit like posttraumatic stress disorder. The couple followed the railroad work to Lawrence, Kansas, but once they arrived, the mister's poor health interfered with his ability to work full days breaking his back over heavy manual labor.

Lucy Hobbs Taylor arrived in Lawrence with her hundred-dollar dentist's chair, her husband, and her dental certificate. When her husband could no longer work on the railroad all the livelong day, Lucy trained him in the art of dentistry and made him a partner. He worked for her as he was able.

When Lucy arrived in Lawrence, it was a small but rapidly growing boomtown in desperate need of skilled people like her. Within four years, she was the proprietor of the most prosperous dental practice in all of Kansas, where she worked side by side with her husband.

The woman who pulled teeth became as famous in Kansas as she had been in Iowa. People came from miles away to see her at her office, the first floor of a two-story house on Massachusetts Street—now the main drag in the still-quaint, ever-thriving college town. She lived upstairs. One of her frequent visitors, a farm wife from just outside of Lawrence by the name of Mrs. George Dolbee, later described Lucy Hobbs Taylor as a "real character" in a letter to the Watkins Community Museum in Lawrence. Every day, Mrs. Dolbee would deliver a pail of milk from her farm to Lucy Hobbs Taylor. And most days, Dr. Taylor would send back the empty pail filled with delicious, homemade potato doughnuts, which she somehow found time to bake between tooth extractions.

Lucy Hobbs Taylor practiced dentistry in Lawrence, Kansas, for forty years and became a prominent member of the community. She mostly treated women and children, but she cared for the occasional male patient as well, and according to one author, "even the bewhiskered pioneers gave her their accolade, 'By Krout, she can pull a tooth as good as a man!'"

She retired temporarily, but couldn't stand the boredom and resumed an active dental practice until the end of her life, telling friends that she was staying just busy enough to keep out of mischief.

Lucy Hobbs Taylor was born in New York, but she wrote in 1892, "I love my adopted country—the West." She was buried in the West, too—in Lawrence, Kansas, her adopted home. And although she had achieved much success in her life, her early struggles remained a painful burden to bear. When later asked about them, she said, "There are passages in all lives where it would be well if the books were closed. Words never explain the heartaches."

By 1900, nearly a thousand women had become dentists. In 1979, the *Wichita Eagle* reported that of the 4,500 women dentists in the United States, only four practiced in Kansas. "But," the reporter noted, "that's a gain of three."

At the root of it all was Lucy Hobbs Taylor, the woman who pulled teeth.

CARRY NATION

(1846–1911)

EVANGELIST, HATCHET WIELDER, SALOON SMASHER, FREQUENT PRISONER

The day after Christmas in the year 1900, a solemn-faced, dark-haired woman wearing a heavy black alpaca dress down to her feet and a black bonnet tied beneath her chin boarded a train to Wichita, Kansas, with a homemade weapon of her own design in hand. If the look on her face and the sense of purpose in her stride did not give away that she meant business, the wooden cane tied to an iron rod certainly should have.

Carry Nation sought to make known, in no uncertain terms, her displeasure with the wanton guzzling of booze in Kansas, supposedly a dry state. Prohibition had been written into the Kansas Constitution in 1881, with the exception that it could be prescribed to "chronic alcoholics" and others for medicinal purposes. A bottle of whiskey distilled and packaged at this time, now on display at the Kansas State Historical Society Museum, boasts not only that it has been medically approved but also that it possesses a "rare delicacy of flavor," as if flavor was of utmost concern to the infirm. So pharmacists often sold alcoholic beverages from the backs of their drugstores, and saloons of the variety you might have seen in old Western movies peddled the stuff shamelessly, right under the noses of law-enforcement agents who simply chose to look the other way.

The night of her arrival, she checked in alone at a no-frills hotel near the train station; she then went around town checking out the joints that were operating in violation of the law. Of the many dens of iniquity she visited that night, the one she encountered at the glamorous Hotel Carey

Carry A. Nation Kansas Historical Society

set off a furor deep inside her. In the lobby, she saw the cherrywood bar, polished to a high shine, more than fifty feet long and curving seductively to form rounded corners. Matching cherry tables were scattered lovingly around it, and a huge barroom mirror glistened above. In her autobiography, she describes the chandeliers overhead as "crystallized tears." But what really got her going, more than the crying lighting fixtures, was the art on display.

A painting of a reclining, nude Cleopatra—replete with delicately styled pubic hair—hung in the bar for all to see. The handmaids fanning her wore only their birthday suits as well. Created by a well-known artist of the time, this painting was the pride and joy of Wichita, and people had rushed to the Hotel Carey to see it immediately upon its installation. Most of them bought drinks at the bar while they were at it, mesmerized by Cleopatra's feminine wiles—and by her other feminine features, too.

Carry Nation had an equal-and-opposite reaction from that of the admiring droves. Far from being lulled by Cleopatra's sultry pose, she was repulsed, and she shrieked aloud upon beholding it.

"Young man, what are you doing here?" she demanded in a rage of the gentleman behind the bar.

"I'm sorry," he is reported to have replied. "We don't serve ladies."

She made clear to the whippersnapper that she did not wish to be served his "hellish poison" and then asked about the painting.

"That's only a picture, madam," the lad offered in reply.

At this point, Carry Nation verbally humiliated the young man, informing him that he was insulting his mother by working in a place that dared display the female form in such a dishonorable way. The youth, not knowing what to say, slipped away into the back of the bar, leaving his extremely disgruntled visitor up front with the handful of paying customers sitting hunched over drinks. Before anyone had a chance to buy her a cocktail, she broke a full bottle of liquor at her feet in a fit of passion and bolted without paying her tab.

Back at the hotel and angry as hell, she upped the ante, weaponwise. She tied an iron ring to the end of the cane-rod and went out hunting for pointy rocks, which she would tote as backup ammo in the morning.

Historians have wondered how she possibly could have marched brazenly toward the Hotel Carey with such heavy and plentiful arsenal in tow and no accomplices to help her shoulder the burden. The standing theory involves large pockets, but definitive answers remain unknown.

What happened next points to the distinct possibility of superhuman wrath, and therefore superhuman strength.

She stepped inside the Hotel Carey, glared at the congregation of seven Wichita men self-medicating before her eyes, and caught the reflection of *Cleopatra at the Bath* in the mirror behind the bar.

Her first move was to hurl a pointy rock at the offending canvas, puncturing a hole in it just below Cleopatra's knee. Then she jettisoned a second rock but did not hit her target, a missed opportunity she continued to regret well into the future. The third rock shattered the expensive mirror that reflected both the fictional scene depicted in the art, and the real-life scene of barroom depravity.

In the midst of her destruction, she cried out, "Peace on earth, good will to men!"—her cane and rod a-swinging all the while.

For Mrs. Nation was a righteous woman.

She was born in Kentucky in November 1846 as Carry Amelia Moore—or perhaps Carrie Amelia Moore. Her parents spelled her name differently in different places, but until she took up saloon smashing—which required a stage name of sorts—she herself opted for Carrie.

She grew up in a log house overlooking the Dix River. A locked cabinet held all the books except the Bible, which sat on a wooden table, always available for casual reading.

Carry was raised by religious and unusual parents. Her father was a businessman and farmer, who appeared to have been lacking in business sense, luck, farming skill, or some combination of these useful traits. Though successful early in his career, he appears to have followed unprofitable opportunities around the Midwest throughout much of Carry's childhood. Though he was a kind man, he was a character. One tale has him converting from one denomination of Christianity to another in his middle age, and seeking baptism in the river. When half-way dunked, he heard his hunting dog alert him to enticing game on the premises and fled his own baptism—still not properly clothed—to hop on his horse and follow it in pursuit.

Say what you will about Mr. Moore: It would have required an unusual man to fill the role of husband to Carry's mother, whose mental illness gave her the peculiar delusion that she was Queen Victoria of England. To maintain this fantasy, when the family rode in a carriage, the driver wore a tall silk hat befitting the driver of royalty, and a slave (for this was the pre–Civil War South) jumped on and off to open and close gates. Mrs. Moore demanded that those around her address her as one would address a queen. Few were inclined to indulge her. She wore purple velvet gowns and a cut-glass crown, far from common accoutrements in Kentucky.

Meanwhile, Carry's grandfather—a deacon of the local Baptist church—was especially fond of brandy and liked to drink it for breakfast. In her memoirs, Carry wrote that every morning when she was a girl, her grandfather would mix sugar, butter, and brandy in a glass and then pour hot water over it. While everyone waited for the morning meal to be served, he would go around the table offering spoonfuls of toddy to children and adults alike. When everyone who was thirsty had taken a sip, he would finish it off himself before taking a morning ride on his horse.

Carry seemed to prefer the company of her household's slaves to the company of her own flesh and blood—understandably enough. At church, where services were segregated, Carry sat with the African Americans in the balcony, where the hymns were sung more spiritedly. The shouting and dancing she encountered in the black sections of the church inspired her early spiritual stirrings.

Carry was prone to stealing, however, and to lying as well—mostly to cover her tracks after stealing something. Stolen objects in her treasure trove included, but were by no means limited to, money, perfume, silk, ribbons, and lace. She committed other acts of blasphemy, too, such as mimicking a preacher while conducting burial services for fallen pets in her yard.

The Moore family hopped around from state to state many times during Carry's childhood, and on one journey from Kentucky to Missouri, Carry came down with a severe illness—diagnosed at the time as "consumption of the bowels"—that laid her up for a year. Her family was worried not only about her possible death but, because she was a known thief and liar, also about what they considered the extremely likely event of her damnation. All efforts to bring her back to good health were accompanied by urgent spiritual teachings—that is, scaring the tar out of the poor girl, just in case treatment proved futile.

At around the same time, she attended a tent revival presided over by an evangelist. Near the end of the revival, after a conversation with the evangelist himself, Carry sat down and wept and wept. "I could not have told anyone what I wept for," she recalled, "except it was a longing to do better."

Some might have seen this redemption as complete, but Carry's family did not. Instead, they sealed the deal by taking the sick girl outside in the cold for a rebaptism ceremony, dunking her in a river with steam rising off of it. She would later write that the girl who went into the water was not the same as the girl who came out. From this point on, Carry reported having visions. She was sick for five more years.

As the Civil War got under way, Carry's father lost livestock, his cotton crops failed, and there was an outbreak of typhoid fever. With everything going on in the border states politically, he went ahead and freed his slaves in 1862. The family now struggled to make ends meet and began taking in boarders.

Carry, a teenager, did chores around the house to keep business running smoothly. She was a good-looking young lady with wavy, long brown hair, glistening almond-shaped eyes, and a little pug nose. She attracted a number of suitors who followed the expected practice of visiting her in her family's parlor. Any time her suitors would try to get personal, she would scare them off by reading aloud from her Bible.

But then she met Dr. Charles Gloyd, a boarder in her parents' home who had recently moved to the area from St. Louis. Carry's mother did not approve of Dr. Gloyd, deeming his common background beneath her standards. She was the Queen of England, after all—or at least, that's who she thought she was. Dr. Gloyd was taken in as a boarder under the condition that under no circumstances would he speak to Carry or sit unchaperoned in a room with her.

We all want what we can't have. Predictably enough, Dr. Gloyd took a shine to Carry and began surreptitiously lending her his collection of Shakespeare's works, leaving love notes tucked away between the pages for her to find. She liked Shakespeare, and she liked the love notes, too. Dr. Gloyd finally kissed the girl in a dark hallway when no one was looking. Carry put her hands to her face and cried that she was ruined, but slowly she gave in to her feelings for Dr. Gloyd.

Her parents were scandalized by the news. Her mother, in particular, seemed to believe that Gloyd was addicted to rum, but Carry—being head over heels in love—either did not believe her mother or did not understand the heartbreak that lay ahead for the bride of a heavy drinker. The couple was soon engaged. To their wedding in November 1867, the groom showed up drunk. Gloyd spent most nights out late, and Carry—desperate and worried—would wander the streets alone, searching for him. Most of the time he could be found at Masonic lodges, and because women were not allowed in these clubhouses, Carry could do nothing but wait for him to stumble home on his own. When Carry found out she was pregnant, she began to panic. Her husband's medical practice had suffered as a result of his drinking, and he wasn't even bringing in enough money to support the two of them, let alone a child.

Her father came to visit her, and found that she was insufficiently fed, poorly clothed, lonely, unhappy, and pregnant. He begged her to come back to the family home. She reluctantly agreed but continued to write her husband letters in an attempt to make things right with him. In one of her letters, she included a pledge not to drink, which she asked him to sign. He did not sign the pledge, and Carry stopped writing to him. When she gave birth to their daughter, Charlien, she did not contact him. It was not until Charlien was six weeks old that Carry went back to the home she had shared with Gloyd to gather her belongings. He begged her to stay, but her parents had urged her to cut off contact with him completely. She loved her husband, but she knew that if Gloyd proved unable to support her and the baby, she would need her parents' help, so she dared not cross them. Carry returned home, and her husband died of pneumonia, with complications resulting from excessive drinking and delirium tremens.

Carry responded with determination to support herself, her mother-in-law, and her daughter. She sold most of the land her father had given her as a wedding present and used the money to build a tiny house for the three of them to share. Then she rented out the house she had lived in with Gloyd and got her certification to become a teacher. She taught for three years and supported her family with a combination of rental money and her teaching salary.

But when she lost her teaching job, she was once again in a serious predicament. At her wit's end, having taken what practical measures she could, she prayed, and what she asked for was a husband. She acknowledged that she had bungled the decision the first time around, and she vowed to trust the selection process to a higher power. Then she waited for a sign.

About ten days later, Carry met David Nation—a lawyer, minister, and journalist—who was just passing through town. When he turned to say something to her, she felt a wave of electricity pass through her body, and she interpreted this as the sign she had anticipated. They were married a few weeks later.

Carry thought the man was handsome, but not many others agreed. David Nation was a tall, thin man who wore a black felt hat and draping black clothes and had a long white beard. His facial expression was twisted and severe.

Any illusion Carry had that this new husband would take care of her was quickly shattered. Instead he moved the family to Texas to pursue a farming venture. In the first year, their horses died, their equipment was destroyed in a feud with neighbors, and most of their money was stolen by a farmhand. David Nation ditched the farm and headed to Columbia, Missouri, making vague promises to look for legal clients. Carry was left to take care of the unprofitable farm by herself and to feed herself, her daughter, Charles Gloyd's mother, and her stepdaughter, Lola Nation. They almost starved to death. Just when things really started looking grim, Carry got a letter from her husband saying he needed money; she took the ailing Mrs. Gloyd, Charlien, and Lola to Columbia to meet David, sold the cotton crop, and got enough money to feed everyone one decent meal.

In an attempt to figure out what she could do to earn some money, Carry stumbled upon a dilapidated old hotel near the railroad. A good Samaritan ditchdigger came forward with a contribution to help her buy the dingy place; without his help, some historians speculate that the family might really have starved.

Carry fixed up the place as best she could and opened for business, welcoming transients in for chump change. She did the cooking and laundry, Lola Nation and Mrs. Gloyd made the beds and straightened up the rooms, and Charlien ran the errands. David Nation spent his days in fruitless pursuit of litigation and spent the evenings dining with hotel guests. The women and girls ate scraps.

Carry started, understandably, to lose it. Her health suffered, anxiety and insomnia overtook her, and she began forgetting things, including her own name. She spent nights staring out the window at a saloon across the way, wondering how her life might be different had the late Dr. Gloyd not allowed himself to be poisoned by drink. And she started having the visions from her childhood once again.

The visions made her spirit expansive, and gave her an unnatural sort of confident serenity. One night, as a fire raged in town and her boarders booked it out of the hotel fearing it would burn to the ground, Carry just sat laughing in a rocking chair, certain that she would not die. The fire was put out right before reaching the hotel. At about this time, she started running around asking people if they loved God, making somewhat of a nuisance of herself and developing a reputation as a loon.

David found a position as a minister, and the family moved to Medicine Lodge, Kansas; Charlien, now married, stayed behind in Missouri. Carry began directing her husband during his sermons, calling out for him to speak more loudly, for example, or telling him when it was time to wrap it up. Her running commentary was audible to the congregation. She also took her message to the streets, seeking out parked buggies where she interrupted couples in danger of getting a little too intimate and stopping well-dressed women in their tracks so she could warn them of the dangers of seduction. This was among her less-popular work. However, at the same time, she took up collections for the poor, distributed coats and shoes to children throughout the county to be sure that no child was unable to attend school, and threw open her doors on Thanksgiving and Christmas, inviting anyone who needed a meal to share her table.

It was in Medicine Lodge that her rage began slowly to focus on alcohol and tobacco. She made a list of all the drugstores and "joints" that openly sold liquor in Medicine Lodge; she stood up in church one Sunday and named them all, one by one. Many people would be content with publicly calling out the offenders, but not Carry Nation. For her, this was just the beginning. Next, she developed and regularly practiced a talent for leveling insults. She would accost people on the street, calling them things like "donkey-faced bedmates of Satan," "makers of drunkards and widows," and "whiskey-swilled, Saturn-faced tosspots."

Her raids on saloons began in Medicine Lodge, where Carry—a furious, umbrella-wielding woman accompanied by an accordion-playing friend—dared to intrude on the sacred turf of men behaving badly, all the while singing "Who Hath Sorrow, Who Hath Woe?"

Crowds gathered to shout equal parts encouragement and harassment. The procession came to a screeching halt at Strong's Saloon, where Mr. Strong himself came barreling out from behind the bar and physically threw Carry out. The crusader found herself flat on the sidewalk in a full-body thud. The town's marshal called out for the fellow to go easy on her, and—having reestablished order—he told Carry Nation that he wished he could take her to jail for the disruption.

"You want to take me, a woman whose heart is breaking to see the ruin of these men, the desolate homes, and broken laws," she protested, "and you a constable oath-bound to close this man's business. Why don't you do your duty?"

The women in the crowd took up her words in a chant: "Do your duty! Do your duty! Do your duty!"

Eventually, the city's officials caved to pressure to close the place, which was all the encouragement the budding revolutionary needed to take her show on the road. Future raids left shattered glass bottles and other telltale debris in their wake. Saloon after saloon closed in the aftermath of her visits.

She next set her sights on the town of Kiowa, on the Oklahoma-Kansas border. This is where she believed the hardened prisoners in the county jail had obtained the liquor that spurred them on to lives of crime. A town of only eight hundred people, Kiowa was home to at least six saloons. Some of the more daring whiskey peddlers in Kiowa were said to make their sales on a door-to-door basis. As she prepared to raid Kiowa saloons alone, she heard the voice of God say unto her, "Take something in your hands to throw at those places and smash them."

Her campaign involved throwing bricks, rocks, bottles, billiard balls, and insults, all hurled with incredible aim and precision at anything breakable. Most of her targets were inanimate objects that shattered ceremoniously, but at the third joint she hit in Kiowa, she threw one of her last pieces of ammo at a young man's head as well. She turned tables on their sides and kicked rungs from chairs. When she finished, she cried out into the night, "Men of Kiowa, I have destroyed three of your places of business! If I have broken a statute of Kansas, put me in jail. If I am not a lawbreaker, your mayor and councilmen are. You must arrest one of us."

A member of city council objected, "Don't you think we can attend to our own business?"

"Yes, you can," she answered glibly. "But you won't."

The predicament faced by law enforcement in Kiowa would replay itself in Kansas town after Kansas town. Carry Nation's behavior was certainly destructive and violent, and officials wanted to toss her in jail to keep the peace. But the private property she destroyed had been put to illegal use, and the businesses she ruined operated in opposition to the law. The city attorney ran around suggesting counts on which the vigilante might be jailed, including "cruelty to a horse." Papers later reported that Mrs. Nation was ultimately fined about a dollar for disturbance of the peace and sent home to Medicine Lodge.

Mrs. Nation gained international notoriety during the course of her saloon-smashing career. By her own account, in sum, she went to jail three times in Wichita, seven times in Topeka, one time in Kansas City, one time in Coney Island, one time in San Francisco, twice in Scranton, once in New Jersey, three times in Pittsburgh, and once in Philadelphia.

She had a lot of fines and bail to pay, not to mention travel expenses, and this is where the weapon of choice that she finally settled on for carrying out her rampages—a spiky metal hatchet, good for puncturing kegs, shattering glass, and hacking up wood tables—really came in handy. It became her calling card, and people associated the visual image of the hatchet with her antisaloon campaign. She began selling miniature souvenir hatchets when she arrived in new towns, and they were so popular that she was able to pay most of her expenses that way for quite some time. Amusingly enough, she even coined a term for the skillful use of the hatchet in wreaking havoc upon saloons: *hatchetation*.

She published a newsletter called *Smasher's Mail*—ironically printed by a saloon owner named Chiles, with whom she appears to have agreed to disagree—and in it, she ran both fan mail and criticism of her tactics. This points to one of the many admirable qualities possessed by Mrs. Nation: Although she had her fair share of flaws—self-righteousness, for example, and uncontrollable rage—she could not be accused of shying away from confrontation or of preaching to the choir. In fact, later in life, she was often booked for speaking engagements, which she accepted even though many of her lectures were of the sideshow variety, meaning that her talks were sandwiched between vaudeville and burlesque acts. Backstage, she tried to win over her fellow performers.

In jail, too, Carry made the unlikeliest friends.

After that smashing campaign in Wichita that started off this chapter, she was thrown into Sedgwick County Jail. The night she was dragged in, she began lecturing her fellow inmates on the dangers of smoking, and asked them to put out their cigarettes because she couldn't stand the foul air. The prisoners balked at this request and then smoked more than ever before in an attempt to suffocate her. She responded in kind, singing hymns at the top of her lungs in an attempt to wear on their nerves. It was a bizarre standoff the likes of which the county jail had probably never seen before, and probably hasn't seen since.

But her irreverence in jail—calling judges "your dishonor" and her insistence that her charge should not be malicious destruction of property but, rather, destruction of malicious property—earned her points with the inmates. She took to addressing them, en masse, as "boys," and they began helping her sort her voluminous mail. They even wrote a poem in her honor.

The man in the cell beside hers—John the Trusty—almost choked Mrs. Nation all on his own that first night with his chimneylike smoking habit. But the two got to know each other, and Carry discovered that John's wife had no means of supporting herself with her husband in jail. Her response was to give him what money she had to pass along to his wife. When a plot developed among law enforcement officials to help Carry "escape," drive her across state line in the dead of night, and kill her, it was John the Trusty who warned her not to leave the jail with these men. Carry heeded John's warning, removed a leg from her cot so she could use it as a weapon and slept on a slanted cot with one eye opened that night. "I know what it is to expect murder in my cell," she later wrote.

As the result of Carry's work, many saloons in Kansas were forced to shut their doors. And the attention she brought to the cause of temperance is undeniable. Some historians make a case that she paved the way for Prohibition. But the author of the book *Whiskey and Wild Women,* Cy Martin, summed up her life's work beautifully when he wrote, "Carry Nation busted up more drinking joints than all the land's rowdy drunks put together," which she surely would have taken as a mighty compliment.

At her last speaking engagement, her memory failed her and she stood, speechless and dumbfounded before the crowd, able only to haltingly say, "I have done what I could." The engraving on her tombstone restates these last words.

SHE HATH DONE WHAT SHE COULD, it reads for all eternity.

MARY ELIZABETH LEASE

(1850–1933)

ADVOCATE FOR THE PEOPLE,
LAWYER FOR THE POOR

"What you farmers need to do is raise less corn and more hell!"
—MARY ELIZABETH LEASE

There is no such thing as notoriety without nicknames.

Mary Elizabeth Lease—who stumped for politicians on the campaign trail before women had won the right to vote—earned more than her fair share of nicknames. Some of the nicknames bestowed upon her were flattering: our Queen Mary of the Alliance and the Joan of Arc of the Populist Party, for example, and Prophetess of the People. Then again, such nicknames as the Red Dragon of Kansas, Yellin' Ellen, the Kansas Pythoness, and Patrick Henry in Petticoats expressed other sentiments entirely.

Mary Lease was known for her radical politics, her unladylike use of language, and her ability to move crowds of struggling farmers with her spellbinding voice. Reports by witnesses claim that she drew not only applause but also tears of anguish and shouts of joy from crowds that gathered when she spoke. But for all the concerned citizens she inspired, she elicited just as strong a response from her detractors, who discredited her by describing her voice as "leather lunged" and having "whiskers on it." One editorialist of the time complimented her, in a backhanded way, for the distinction of being able to sing bass in a choir.

Mary Lease studied the law—not in law school but on her own—and was admitted to the bar in 1885. She provided legal counsel to people

Mary Elizabeth Lease Kansas Historical Society

who could not afford it. But she never charged her clients for services rendered, and on these grounds she did not consider herself a lawyer. She stumped for politicians but never ran for elected office, and she did not possess the right to vote. She supported and turned against politicians based on personal conviction and not party allegiance and, therefore, was not a politician in the strictest sense of the word.

She wrote for newspapers but never claimed objectivity and was not paid for her commentaries, satires, and poems (at least early in her writing career, in Kansas, she was not paid). In fact, it was not until the latter part of her career that she would have dared to call herself a professional writer, though she was certainly a published writer. It was her spoken words, not her written words, that made her famous.

Attempting to answer the question of what it was she might call herself exactly, when asked this very question during an interview conducted retrospectively at age seventy, Mary Lease settled, after some hesitation, on "advocate."

Born in 1850, Mary was the sixth child of Irish immigrant parents living in Pennsylvania. She was a good student and loved reading. She graduated at fifteen and became a teacher close to home. Teachers' salaries at the time were quite low, however, and women earned even less than men, which irked Mary and prompted her to try to organize her colleagues to demand higher wages. When this effort proved unsuccessful, the young woman made up her mind to venture westward to Kansas—as so many settlers were doing at the time—because she had heard that teachers earned a better salary in the Midwest. Upon her arrival in Kansas in 1870, the impossibly tall woman with soft blue eyes, wavy hair, and an athlete's agile gait landed on a Kansas farm, where she witnessed the hardships of the rural West firsthand before securing a position as a teacher at a Catholic school for girls in the fall of 1871. Her time on a Kansas farm, though brief, was difficult, and the difficulty would be forever emblazoned in her heart and mind.

In 1873, she married a Kansas man by the name of Charles Lease, a pharmacist who ran his own drugstore. Charles was a respected businessman who made a successful run for mayor shortly after he and Mary were married. In short order, Mary did what was expected of her; that is to say, she gave birth to six children in the span of eleven years. Of those six children, four survived—a survival rate that would not have been uncommon at the time. As biographer Dorothy Rose Blumberg wrote in the Kansas State Historical Society's *Kansas History* journal, "the young mother seemed to accept the cycle of pregnancy, birth—and only too often death—as a woman's appointed lot."

The life of a housewife in sparsely populated Kingman County was assuredly lonely. Mary spent her days baking bread, cleaning house, and worshipping at church. But while she kneaded dough and washed dishes, pinned to the wall in front of her was usually a newspaper article of particular interest. Thanks to her great ability to multitask, she developed an unparalleled command of the issues of her day. Her household obligations did nothing to abate her hunger for knowledge, nor did they prevent her from satisfying that hunger—privately anyway.

Mary's earliest speaking engagements were on behalf of the causes of temperance and labor. Her eloquence was quickly noted, and according to reports, quite surprising. It was in the growing labor movement that Mary became not just a speaker but also an organizer. But speaking was her true love, and she spoke in favor of a handful of causes near and dear to her heart, ranging from Ireland's struggle for independence to the plight of the impoverished to the legal status of women.

Having caught the bug for public speaking, she branched out, turning her efforts toward suffrage—the growing movement in favor of a woman's right to vote. In general, Mary could not stomach the commonly held belief that a woman's intellect was inferior to a man's. "There is no difference," she told crowds, "between the mind of an intelligent woman and the mind of an intelligent man." She also spoke against the prevailing assumption that women were represented by the votes cast by their husbands, reminding crowds of the significant number of women who did not have husbands and who, therefore, did not have any representation at all.

But it was not until she took up the plight of the Kansas farmer and became a known figure in the Populist Party that her celebrity status took Kansas and, indeed, the entire country by storm.

This might be a good time to say a few words about what was happening in rural Kansas during the second half of the nineteenth century, just as Mary Elizabeth Lease arrived on the scene.

In the 1860s, Kansas had scarcely been settled, in large part because the pioneers believed the territory's climate and soil to be utterly worthless due to a lack of rainfall. Early pioneers' assessment of Kansas was that it had nothing to offer but "flat land, no trees, and snakes." The perception of the West—and of Kansas in particular—was that it was part of the Great American Desert—not a bountiful land where a farmer might seek his fortune. As a result, Kansas was a huge plot of land that attracted only a miniscule population for quite some time.

A couple of laws passed in the 1860s finally brought settlers to Kansas in significant numbers.

First, there was the Homestead Act. Passed in 1862, the Homestead Act made it possible for anyone over twenty-one years of age who had filed the intention to become a United States citizen and who had not borne arms against the United States to acquire a 160-acre plot of unsettled government land by living on it, building a twelve-by-fourteen-foot dwelling on the land, and making improvements to the land for five years. Veterans of the Civil War who fought for the Union could subtract the number of years of service from the residency requirements.

In 1863, the Pacific Railway Act came into law to facilitate and encourage the construction of railroad and telegraph lines from the Missouri River to the Pacific Ocean. This law gave railway companies the right of way to lay down tracks, and it also granted the companies plots of land for every mile of track they laid. The railroad companies could turn around the land for profit, and then use the money generated by land sales to fund the construction of more railroads.

Funding was essential for the railroad companies, but perhaps even more important was getting people to move to unsettled territories. After all, if nobody moved to the areas surrounding the railroads, what use would the railroads be? Who would want to travel from here to there if all that's *there* is tumbleweed? Why would anyone ship goods to the West if the West possessed neither stores nor customers, neither commerce nor industry? Populating the West was crucial to the success of the railroad companies.

So just as the government made the land available to the railroad companies, the railroad companies turned around and made that land available to the people—most of whom had very little cash. The railroad companies started selling land on credit, to be paid back over time. They offered what they called long credit and short credit. Short credit was for people who believed that they could pay off the land in three years. Long credit allowed settlers to pay for their land over the course of ten years. Long credit was encouraged based on the accepted wisdom of the time that any money a newly relocated farmer had would best be spent on the purchase of tools, the construction of a home, and the improvement of the land. The railroad companies tacked on other little perks, too. Some paid entire families' rail fares, bringing families west and footing the bill.

At the same time, railroad companies put out brochures and pamphlets advertising the great things settlers would find upon arriving in their new western homes. They recounted the tales of earlier settlers who had come to the West with nothing and, in just a few years, achieved great success and were now living lives of comfort and abundance. They also reminded potential settlers of the Homestead Act, since they cared not so much about making money from land sales as about populating the territory by any means necessary. In addition, they attempted to discredit the notion that rainfall was sparse in western states. Brochures quoted impressive rainfall statistics and described lush, green settings as part of what we might now call an advertising blitz.

In 1873, another law known as the Timber Culture Act gave the West yet another public relations boost. The Timber Culture Act allowed homesteaders to get an additional plot of land by agreeing to set aside a significant amount of land to plant trees.

News of heavy rains and bountiful harvests, in addition to the suddenly very real opportunity for common folk to acquire land (and plenty of it), got the intended response. Over the course of the 1870s, the population of Kansas grew from a third of a million to a million, and it continued to grow through much of the 1880s.

In truth, rainfall *was* abundant in the summer months in Kansas during the late 1870s and early 1880s. As fate would have it, however, this was not typical of Kansas summers. The railroad companies' advertising—though false—was not knowingly false. A fluke was more like it. The population growth of the 1870s was concentrated in the eastern portion of the state. In the 1880s, the settlers pushed further into the usually arid western portion of Kansas. People came, and money followed—not their own money, because those lured westward were typically people without means, but the money of investors who made loans to the settlers willing to do the legwork. Boomtowns popped up throughout Kansas. The towns built their own schools and roads by going into debt. Community leaders assumed that growing populations would result in greater tax revenue down the road, and that the money coming in through taxes would pay off the debt.

That's when the rainfall returned to normal levels in 1887. Settlers experienced their first midwestern drought, and they had not learned to farm the land under these conditions. People began to head back east in covered wagons, some of which bore slogans like "In God we trusted, in Kansas we busted."

For those who stayed, a struggle lay ahead.

Prices for crops had fallen, and the cost to ship food via railroad to cities where people might buy it was high. Farmers in Kansas complained that it cost a bushel of corn to send a bushel of corn to market.

Railroads, too, began operating at a loss. They had expanded too fast and too far, laying tracks in areas that had not grown dense with population, as anticipated. Support for struggling railroads was written into state constitutions, and taxpayers shouldered the burden of keeping them afloat.

Kansas farmers grew resentful of railroad companies, banks, and mortgage companies. The term *Wall Street* came to represent all of these interests rolled into one.

Farmers who had prospered upon arriving in Kansas now faced a daunting combination of failing crops, low prices for their wares, high taxes, and imminent foreclosures. Frustration on the frontier brought many farmers to their breaking point.

Mary Lease, meanwhile, always dressed in black. This was not a fashion statement. During the drought, it was hard to come by water with which to launder garments, so she wore black in hopes that the stains on her clothes would not be so obvious.

She had worked on a farm in Kingman for less than a year, but it was enough to qualify her for membership in the Farmers' Alliance— a movement that worked to improve conditions for midwestern food producers. In 1888, the disgruntled farmers and disgruntled laborers joined forces to form the Union Labor Party. They held a convention in Wichita to come up with a political agenda, and when Mary Lease spoke to pledge her support, the *Wichita Daily Eagle* reported that her speech was followed by "wild cheers that lasted several minutes."

She was a fiery speaker, though her demeanor—when not speaking before a crowd—was supposedly lifeless and demure. Onlookers marveled that it was as though she was a woman possessed when behind the podium.

In 1889, a convention was held to draw up a set of demands on behalf of the People's Party, or Populist Party as it came to be known. These demands were sent to Kansas politicians. When Senator John J. Ingalls did not respond, the party's agenda became preventing his reelection. Mary Lease became one of the main speakers on behalf of this agenda. Over the next several months, her speaking engagements took her all over the state, sometimes requiring her to make more than one speech in a day—and not necessarily in the same town. It was a rigorous schedule. Still, she made it a point never to be away from her family for longer than two weeks at a time. When trips were short, she tried to take one of her children along with her.

In 1890, Mary Lease made more than 160 speeches for the Populist cause, taking banks, railroads, and mortgage companies to task.

"Wall Street owns the country," she said in one of her more famous speeches. "It is no longer a government of the people, by the people, and for the people, but a government of Wall Street, by Wall Street, and for Wall Street. . . ."

"You may call me an anarchist, a Socialist, or a Communist," she yelled out in another speech. "I care not, but I hold to the theory that if one man has not enough to eat three times a day and the other man has twenty-five million dollars, that last man has something that belongs to the first."

In yet another speech recounted in a 1935 article that ran in the *Kansas City Times,* she said to a crowd of agitated farmers, "You farmers were told two years ago to raise a big crop. Well, you did and what became of it? Eight-cent corn, ten-cent oats, two-cent beef, and no price at all for butter and eggs—that's what came of it. Then the politicians said we suffered from overproduction. Yet ten thousand children starve to death every year in the United States. The common people are robbed to enrich their masters."

Them's fightin' words. But it was not until she told the crowd to raise "less corn and more hell" that people really got riled up. The moment is described in a novel titled *The Heritage of the Bluestem: A Romance of the Prairies*. Novelist Anna Matilda Carlson sets the scene this way in her story: "On the eve of the election, Mary Elizabeth Lease, prophetess of the people . . . spoke. . . . Painting a lurid picture of Wall Street reaching out its tentacles of gold to strangle farmers, the speaker, by the sheer magnetism of her personality, worked the audience into a frenzy. . . . The crowd went wild. Men leaped upon the seats and waved their arms. They were shouting, singing. Women laughed hysterically, or wept."

Although Populism never held much sway in national elections, it was persuasive and powerful in Kansas, and Senator Ingalls was summarily defeated, as hoped. Mary Lease congratulated the women of Kansas, giving them credit for the favorable turn of events, and gloated publicly in victory. In response, John Ingalls told the press, "Only Indians and women scalp the dead."

This was not the last of the criticisms Mary Lease heard in response to her vocal stances on political issues. When she campaigned in the South with Populist presidential candidate James B. Weaver in 1892, becoming the first woman to address the state legislature in Georgia, angry mobs armed with rocks and eggs tried to intimidate her from speaking. *The Greensboro Daily Record* reported that a woman traveling around the country making political speeches was "simply disgusting," adding that "Southern manhood revolts at the idea of degrading womanhood to the level of politics." (Weaver, it should be noted, was not particularly well received in the South himself, and Mary Lease later mused that southern chivalry in Georgia made "a regular walking omelet" of him.)

Back in Kansas, Mary Lease became a delegate of the Populist Party's state convention, where she proposed an equal suffrage amendment, which was eventually adopted by the party. After that year's election, rumors spread that Mary Lease would run for a seat in the United States Senate. Women across the country—including Susan B. Anthony—expressed their support, but Mary Lease insisted she was not a candidate. She instead worked to assist farmers in the event of foreclosure.

When eventually the Populist Party's politics became more mainstream and its adherents once again attached their sympathies to either the Democratic or Republican party, Mary Lease gave up politics for the most part, left her estranged husband, and moved to New York City. There, she was hired by Joseph Pulitzer, who needed writers for his newspaper, *New York World.* She covered politics for the paper and was sent to the national political conventions with hotel accommodations and decent pay. Of her tenure at *New York World,* Mary Lease told a *Kansas City Star* interviewer, "Never before in my life had I received such generous treatment." Her career in journalism allowed her to buy her own home and put three of her four children through college. During her New York period, she resumed her unofficial practice of the law, renting a small dingy office in lower Manhattan and providing counsel to the poor free of charge. In her spare time, she wrote a book with the humorously bold title, *The Problem of Civilization Solved.*

Mary Lease's goal, in studying politics and the law, was actually to prepare herself for the presidency. Or so she said many years later. More than a century after Mary Lease set aside this dream, it is still the case that no woman has been elected president of the United States.

"In that position," she said, "I could have been the advocate of the poor man politically and economically. But I soon learned the only gift I had was forensic eloquence. . . . So I gave up my aim of being the advocate of the people from high political office and decided to devote my life to doing what good I could."

But Mary Lease's involvement in politics was far from inconsequential. Although the Populist Party's influence was both short-lived and geographically limited, many of its tenets have since been adopted: public ownership of public utilities, for example, as well as women's suffrage and the direct election of senators.

"The seed we sowed in Kansas," she proclaimed, "did not fall on barren ground."

At seventy years of age, Mary Lease still wore all black, and her hair had not grayed.

LILLA DAY MONROE

(1858–1929)
SUFFRAGIST AND JOURNALIST, COUNTING WOMEN'S VOTES AND STORIES

When she crept up to her grandmother's attic, Joanna Stratton didn't expect to find anything unusual. It was winter of 1975, and she was visiting her grandmother in Kansas while on break from Harvard. In all probability, she was bored.

Time moves slowly in the Midwest, especially when it's bitterly cold outside. When the air outside gets so cold it practically burns the skin to the touch, the whole world—for comfort's sake—shrinks down to the size of your home, where you can sit by the fire or burrow under a blanket with a cup of hot cocoa. So, with her world shrunk down to the size of an old Victorian home, Joanna went exploring upstairs.

It was something she always did when visiting her grandmother, this snooping around among tattered old ball gowns and once-fashionable hats, scanning titles of tattered books and magazines on dusty shelves, thumbing through boxes of family letters and silvery black-and-white photographs, opening trunks and drawers and cabinets to see what awaited her there. This was a day like any other day that Joanna had spent with relatives in Kansas.

Surely she must have known that her great-grandmother, the one who built this house in 1887, was a person of note in Kansas history. No doubt the family was proud that Lilla Day Monroe had been the first woman to practice law before the Kansas Supreme Court, that she had been a real spitfire and lobbied to have a statue dedicated to the memory of hardy pioneer women on the grounds of the Kansas State Capitol. The statue, still standing to this day, depicts a cloaked woman kneeling

Lilla Day Monroe Kansas Historical Society

with an infant in one arm, the other arm wrapped around a studying boy, and a rifle slung across her knee. Her clothing drapes over her in a way that almost deifies her. This statue, Joanna must have known, was her grandmother's idea.

But she didn't go snooping through the attic looking for history with a capital *H*. She was just exploring, as we all do in grandparents' attics and basements, searching for clues about who our grandparents were before they were grandparents, who our parents were before they were parents, and, if we're lucky and our families have stayed in one place for long enough as Joanna's had, maybe even who our great-grandparents were before they were anything at all.

While indulging in this habitual time travel on that particular winter day, however, the dark-haired scholar stumbled upon the kind of thing scholars always dream of stumbling upon. She opened an old filing cabinet that had been pushed into a corner. Ducking her head to squeeze into the tight space, she began skimming the yellowing papers inside. She had just found the personal stories of eight hundred Kansas pioneer women, written in their own words. In her introductory remarks for *Pioneer Women: Voices from the Kansas Frontier*, Stratton wrote:

> *It was an exhilarating moment of discovery for me. As I sat poring over the carefully penned writings, a human pageantry came alive for me. . . . I shivered with Emma Brown in her rain-soaked soddy. I watched Hannah Hoisington defend a neighbor's cabin against a pack of wolves and marveled as Jenny Marcy confronted a stampede of Texas longhorns. I celebrated Christmas day with little Harriet Adams and joined in a polka with lighthearted Catherine Cavender. I saw Anna Morgan held hostage by the Cheyenne. I witnessed Mrs. Lecleve endure childbirth alone in her cabin. I sang hymns with Lydia Murphy Toothaker and campaigned for woman suffrage with the Reverend Olympia Brown.*

Lilla Day Monroe had believed, correctly, that one day, people would care to know how these hardy women lived and endured in the state's earliest days. The cowboy and the railroad worker and the bootlegger and the soldier had all been hallowed and mythologized. Nobody had asked, just yet, what women had been up to all that time. But she knew, or maybe just hoped, that one day surely someone would. She suspected, however, that it might be too late to get answers, so she took it upon herself to ask the questions and to preserve the answers so that when people got around to asking, these eight hundred answers would exist.

She placed her original call for Kansas pioneer women's personal memoirs in a magazine she edited. Her intent was simply to run the responses in that very magazine's pages. She did publish a few of the stories that way, but quickly realized that the flood of responses merited more than a series of magazine stories, which ran the risk of being printed today and forgotten tomorrow. She decided to continue compiling stories and then to dedicate herself to organizing the material for an eventual book. She quit her substantial work outside the home to focus her efforts on this project full-time. Her mail was never boring. It contained heartache and triumph, suffering and redemption, once-ordinary details of a kind of daily life nearly forgotten by the early twentieth century. But Lilla got sick, and in 1929, she died before this grand opus ever saw print. Her great-granddaughter, Joanna Stratton, would complete and publish that book sixty-one years later, inspired by that fateful day spent rummaging in Lilla's attic.

Lilla Day Monroe was born in Indiana in 1858 and came to Kansas in 1884—at the tail end of what is now known as the "frontier era." She settled in Wakeeney, a western Kansas settlement created by pioneers traveling westward in search of better lives for themselves and their families. Many of them stopped about where Lilla stopped, at the midpoint between Kansas City and Denver, Colorado.

In short order, she met, fell in love, and married Lee Monroe, an attorney. Not only did she keep home and raise four children; she also clerked in her husband's law office. At home, she spent many grueling years stealing moments for her own study of the law. Eventually, she passed the bar exam. In 1895, Lilla Day Monroe became the first woman to practice before the Kansas Supreme Court. Knowing the law and the Constitution was important to her as she tirelessly championed what she believed to be the great causes of women—in particular, the cause of suffrage.

Her interest in the rights of women was sparked by a fairly ordinary scene that left a strong impression on her when she was just a little girl. On a visit to the general store, she happened to witness a disturbing scene.

A couple stood near the counter, and the woman asked the man if she could have a dollar. "To buy what?" the man asked. The woman explained that she needed a few things: some gingham, an apron. The other shoppers, like Lilla, could not help but eavesdrop. They became curious as to whether the woman would be given the dollar. Apparently, they did not do a very good job of pretending not to listen. The man realized he had an audience and played to it. Holding out the dollar, he quickly yanked it away as soon as his wife reached for it. When she realized she was being held up for ridicule, the woman began to cry—and so did Lilla. She would remember this story for the rest of her life.

In September 1906, she gave a talk on the history of the woman suffrage movement. In Kansas, at this time, women had the right to vote in municipal elections. This right had been granted decades earlier. And yet Kansas had not yet given its women the right to vote above and beyond the municipal level, and the United States had not yet granted universal suffrage.

Lilla began her speech frankly. "Before entering upon this history, I think it is my right to establish some sort of comradeship between myself and the gentlemen present by telling them just how it happens that I was chosen to make them miserable."

She went on. "No woman wants to talk on woman suffrage to a man. It is inevitable that the man should feel aggrieved. . . . You will go away feeling that I have said unpleasant things, and my committee that handed me the topic will not be able to help me bear the burden of your displeasure."

Lilla proceeded to relieve the men in her audience of any guilt the subject of woman suffrage might have caused them to feel, explaining that it was she and her sisters in arms whose responsibility it was to demand change. "[These] conditions are, have been, and will continue so long as women do not object."

And object Lilla did. She claimed that the vote was like the dollar that the woman in the general store had requested. She believed that women were being ridiculed for asking for something to which they had a basic, absolute right, and that for unfair reasons, only men could grant it. She argued that economic power and the right to vote were intertwined—that so long as women couldn't vote, politicians did not have much motivation to defend them. And she argued that the right to vote in municipal elections was only a few cents of the full dollar requested.

She fought for women's causes, not only as a lawyer and a speaker, but also as a journalist. She started and edited two magazines: *The Club Women* and *The Kansas Women's Journal*. And it was for these magazines that she began her project of recording and saving the stories of other pioneer women.

Teachers described the conditions trying to educate youth in a territory where school districts and formal public education systems had not yet been established, and where—for a time—schoolhouses had not been built. Textbooks could not be easily or cheaply shipped to rural areas, and teachers relied on whatever books the children were able to gather from their homes—often just tattered Bibles. Some taught in dugouts with dirt floors and walls, burlap hanging between the students and the walls so that the children would not go home covered in dirt. The students sat on benches. The teacher had no chalkboard.

Others taught in spare rooms of their own homes, or in students' houses; at the time, it was not unusual for teachers to live with students for a time, teach lessons, and then move on to the next home in the village. The funds did not exist to pay them well enough to secure their own lodgings, so this approach solved two problems at once. Teachers seemed to start working at around age sixteen or seventeen, and most were women simply because so few other opportunities were open to them. One teacher who submitted her memoirs boldly asserted that one-third of the women in Kansas at some point taught school. If the women included in this book are in any way representative, she was lowballing her estimate.

Lilla collected stories from farm wives confessing loneliness and isolation, and women who as young girls had helped their fathers out in the fields as well as their mothers inside the homes. She heard from a woman who had grown up in Abilene, where cattle stampeded as the guard dog lay snoring and her mother fainted from terror, leaving the girl to her own devices as she did her very best to wrangle the thousand or so bovines alone. There were women who hid from border ruffians during the Civil War years, and one whose mother went about town with a gun demanding that the pro-slavery man who wanted to kill her husband show himself so she could give him a piece of her mind, and maybe more.

Lilla's greatest accomplishment, perhaps, was to know how brave and strong the other women were in her midst, and to think their bravery and strength mattered enough that history might want to take note.

All eight hundred manuscripts she collected and organized were later typed by her daughter. After her great-granddaughter Joanna finished writing the book Lilla had been preparing to write herself, the complete collection of stories was donated to the Kansas State Historical Society, where students of history can still enjoy reading them today.

Susanna Madora Salter

(1860–1961)

THE ACCIDENTAL MAYOR OF ARGONIA

They say well-behaved women rarely make history. Susanna Madora Salter, the first woman ever to be elected mayor of a United States city, is a notable exception.

Then again, maybe she didn't make history at all. Maybe history made her. Either way, it's safe to say that Mrs. Salter didn't *mean* to make history. She stumbled into it. There she was, just living peacefully and quietly in the small Quaker township of Argonia, Kansas, minding her own business, when all of a sudden, out of nowhere, history snatched her up without consulting her and borrowed her life for a year.

To her credit, when history came for her, Mrs. Salter went along with it. She did what history expected of her by doing what nobody had ever expected of her—or any woman—before. She served as mayor, though that had never been her plan.

Her name was added to the ballot by a handful of pranksters hoping to embarrass her.

The year was 1887, and women had just been granted the right to vote in municipal elections in Kansas. At the time, this was considered a radical experiment in female suffrage. Eager to exercise their newfound political leverage, the women of Argonia got together to agree upon a list of preferred candidates in the upcoming election. The idea was to distribute the list to the women who would be voting for the first time. A group of women had already been assembling for Women's Christian Temperance Union meetings; they simply built upon the existing organization, using its infrastructure to reach out to new voters in large numbers. The group's regular leader was unable

Susanna Madora Salter Kansas Historical Society

to attend the meeting, and by sheer luck of the draw, Susanna Madora Salter—known to her friends as Dora—ran the meeting in her place. As a result, she was singled out as the target of some rather mean-spirited practical jokes.

A group of conservative men in town, believing politics to be theirs and theirs alone, sought to put a stop to the madness. That women had earned the right to vote was one thing, but now they were talking about electing candidates who would represent their interests. The women were taking things just a little too far. At least, that's how the pranksters saw things.

They began taunting Dora face to face at the big meeting she presided over. Two of the men attended the meeting uninvited and heckled the women throughout the proceedings. When this proved ineffective, they met—twenty strong—at a little Argonia restaurant, where they devised a plan to counter and mock the women. Their scheme was to nominate a slate of candidates identical to the women's list of preferred candidates, with only one difference: Where the women had listed the name of a man for mayor, the men listed Susanna Madora Salter. They were able to add her name to the ballots because, at that time, candidates did not have to file in person before election day. Anyone could nominate anyone.

Their assumption was that the women would show up at the polls so well prepared to vote for the candidates endorsed at the meeting that they would not even notice Mrs. Salter's name on the ballot. They would vote, instead, for the male candidate they had selected and approved in advance of the big day—their first day admitted to the polls. The men in town, of course, would not think of voting for a woman—or so the conspirators reasoned. The gag was that when Susanna Madora Salter secured only a handful of votes, the landslide defeat would send a message to the women in town that their participation in politics was a complete joke. They figured it would be such an embarrassment that women would refrain from trying to get involved again in the future.

Early on the morning of election day, the first voters to do their civic duty were surprised to see Mrs. Salter's name listed as an option. Mr. Salter, the candidate's husband, was particularly surprised, as his wife had not shared any plans to run for office. She hadn't expressed even the slightest interest in running for office over dinner, inside the home, and she certainly hadn't campaigned outside the home.

For her part, Mrs. Salter was at home doing everyday chores when suddenly, a delegation arrived to inform her she was running for mayor. They had gotten to the bottom of the prank, explained it to her, and asked her if she would be willing to serve a term in office—should she be elected. If not, they graciously informed her that her name could be removed from the ballots.

Susanna Madora Salter thought it over. She hadn't particularly wanted to be mayor, but she agreed, her hands still drying from doing the wash, that if elected, she would faithfully carry out her duties. She immediately set about putting a last-minute campaign together. It couldn't hurt.

Her husband arrived home in a huff shortly thereafter and was shocked to hear of her plans not only to serve if elected, but in fact, to spend the day leading a get-out-the-vote effort rather than quietly accepting the humiliation intended for her.

Later that afternoon, she went to the polls with her parents. It was her first time voting. It was her first day running for office. And until just a few hours earlier, she hadn't had any inkling that her name would appear on this first ballot she would ever cast. It was a lot to take in.

Ever the prim and proper lady, Mrs. Salter voted for the Women's Christian Temperance Union candidates all the way down the line, but she did not vote for any candidate in the mayoral race. She left that line blank. To vote for herself would have been such an undignified move. Even without voting for herself, she won the election by a two-thirds majority.

On April 4, 1887, Susanna Madora Salter woke up having never so much as cast a vote. By the end of the day, not only had she voted; she had also discovered she was a candidate, launched her first political campaign, and won her first political victory. She woke up thinking about housework and went to bed as mayor.

All in all, it was a pretty big day.

April 4, 1887, was actually a big day for women all over Kansas, who—like Susanna—had never voted before and suddenly had the option of heading to the polls.

A quick read of the two newspapers published in Kansas City at that time reveals a variety of responses to the big doings in Argonia. In some cities, turnout among women had dramatic effects on election results, while in other places, women pretty much stayed home in spite of having been granted the right to vote. But newspaper coverage of elections across the state conveys an attitude of disbelief—of excitement mixed with uncertainty. People had their eyes on these municipal elections. They tried to imagine whether politics in Kansas and beyond were about to change for good. And if so, *how?*

The following headlines come straight out of the *Kansas City Times* and the *Kansas City Journal:* SENSIBLE EMPORIA WOMEN OUT, WICHITA WOMEN STAY AT HOME, EMPORIA LADIES NOT HAPPY, LOVELY WOMEN DEFEATED, THE LADIES INTERESTED, THE LADIES RUN RUSSELL, and ABILENE WOMEN HEARD FROM.

This represents just a small selection of the headlines turning readers' attention to the experiment of limited female suffrage in Kansas. Most of the state's election coverage discussed whether women voted, in what quantities they voted, and to what effect. Very little election coverage addressed such matters as which party prevailed based on what sorts of campaign promises, for example, or the expected impact of the election on the everyday lives of Kansans. The gender breakdown of voters was, without a doubt, the hot-button issue in 1887.

The spirit of the day's proceedings was all over the map. In Hutchinson, women enthusiastically campaigned from buggies, and their vote was split about fifty-fifty. Two hundred or so Hutchinson women turned out, in all.

The story in Wichita—the biggest city in Kansas—unfolded quite differently. Out of six hundred women who registered to vote, only about one hundred actually voted. "Women of ill repute were the first and foremost in the exercise of their newly acquired right," the *Kansas City Journal*'s reporter was quick to point out, suggesting that women who voted were somehow sullied by the act. "There were, however, many women of respectability who stood in the line of voters," the small news item allowed.

By contrast, the newspaper's staff credited Ottawa women with domesticating life at the polls. "The presence of ladies today at the polls as voters, for the first time in the history of Ottawa, had a mellowing influence, and the city has had its quietest election ever held here." Not only that, but these well-behaved women knew how to follow the rules better than their male counterparts, according to reports. "The ladies voted 400 strong and as a rule went to the polls without escort. . . . Most of the ladies came prepared with ballots, and the judges report a less number of errors in their especial ballot boxes than in those of males."

Election coverage in Paola focused on the emotional state of the first-time voters, and not so much on the impact of their vote. The writer expressed concern for the well-being of the so-called gentler sex in the rough-and-tumble world of political enfranchisement. "Election day dawned bright and clear, and among the first to vote were the ladies, who cast their maiden vote today. The ladies naturally acted a little timid at first, but they finally braced their work, and took courage as they worked."

Of all the Kansas towns covered, Leavenworth and Emporia seem to have borne witness to the most dramatic confrontations between those who favored women's suffrage, and those who opposed it. In both cities, black women showed up to cast their ballots alongside white women. This was an unexpected turn of events, and the populations of the towns where it happened did not react calmly.

In Emporia, said the *Kansas City Journal*, "wives of prominent citizens, leaders of society, models of propriety and meekness were seen driving frantically toward the polls, their costly silks and satins mingling with the coarse rags of some colored representative of the female voting populace, or of some degraded outcast whose only virtue was that she had a vote. . . . Not a few encounters of a fistic nature between prominent citizens took place that day." The reporter took further glee in acknowledging that the outcome of the election had not favored the women's preferred candidates.

In Leavenworth, where black women also attempted to lay claim to their right to vote—presenting themselves first and foremost as women, regardless of race or skin color—news reports actually went so far as to compare the black women to livestock. The reporter claimed that they were "placed in carriages and driven to the polls, where they were voted like so many cattle."

The day that Susanna Madora Salter was elected mayor in the teeny-tiny town of Argonia, women in the state of Kansas had secured a limited right to vote. But their place in politics, even as voters, was far from secure. It was scary, it was exciting, it was a prize that some women cherished and others admired or even just acknowledged from afar. It was in this climate that Dora accepted the duties of mayor.

On the sixth of April, Dora received official notice that she had, in fact, been elected mayor. It arrived in the form of a short letter, sent by mail:

Madam,

You are hereby notified that at an election held in the city of Argonia on Monday, April 4/87, for the purpose of electing city officers, you were duly elected to the office of Mayor of said city. You will take due notice thereof, and govern yourself accordingly.

Of the five city council members also elected that day, two had been among the pranksters who—intending to humiliate Mrs. Salter out of political participation—had actually catapulted her *into* it in a historically significant manner.

On her first day leading a city council meeting, she showed up and addressed the men. "Gentlemen," she proclaimed, striking a tone at once authoritative and humble. "What is your pleasure? You are the duly elected officials of this town. I am merely your presiding officer."

This set the tone for a harmonious year in city politics. Far from changing Argonia forever, Dora's term was totally and completely uneventful. No new ordinances were passed. The council arrested some conductors of horse-driven wagons who had neglected to procure licenses. The council also issued a warning to some boys in town who had been caught throwing rocks at a vacant house. It takes a pretty quiet year in city hall for actions like these to remain on the books as defining moments.

A correspondent for the *New York Sun* was sent to Argonia to see what the fuss was about, and report back about how things were going under supposed "petticoat rule" out West. The correspondent let his readers know that they would be hard-pressed to find much out of the ordinary happening at the city council meetings in Argonia, with the exception that the mayor was a woman. The reporter made note of how Dora dressed, and mentioned that aside from curtailing conversations she determined to be irrelevant to the matters at hand, she didn't intervene a great deal in the proceedings, making her a rather effective leader. He compared the city councilmen's attitude toward her to that of schoolboys toward an unpopular teacher. They were begrudgingly well behaved in her presence.

At this particular meeting, one of the city councilmen suggested that the cost of a license to operate a billiards table be reduced so it might be more affordable for ordinary citizens. Mayor Salter calmly noted that the town was not in dire need of more billiards tables than it already possessed, thereby disqualifying this as an urgent matter for the council's attention. Another councilman agreed with her, and the subject was dropped. So went life in Argonia under "petticoat rule."

The reporter also followed Mrs. Salter around town to see what life was like for her there. "The mischievous young boys regard her much as a New York gamin does a 'cop,' and 'There's the Mayor!' is often the signal for a general scattering of urchins as she approaches." More cities in Kansas elected female mayors—ones who ran for office on purpose—the following year.

Even Mr. Salter, who was skeptical and enraged when he initially saw his wife's name on the ballot, got used to the arrangement. In fact, he got a real kick out of referring to himself the husband of the mayor whenever the opportunity presented itself.

Mrs. Salter did not develop a deep and abiding love for politics during that year in office. If she did, she hid it well. The *New York Sun* reporter claims to have asked her if she had any ambition to work in female suffrage circles or to remain involved in civic affairs.

"No, indeed," she told him without missing a beat. "I shall be very glad when my term in office expires, and shall be only too happy to thereafter devote myself entirely, as I have always done heretofore, to my family."

And, though it is rare for a politician to stand by her word, Mrs. Salter never did take back this promise: She never ran for elected office again.

But her one year in office is still memorialized, to this very day, on a mural near Argonia's town square. She stands among sunflowers, in the fields where she used to walk to clear her head. Because, let's face it: Argonia has never been so famous as it was in 1887, the year it elected the first female mayor in the United States, all thanks to a practical joke that backfired and changed history forever.

Ann Clarke

(1812–?)

ESCAPED SLAVE, SEEKER OF FREEDOM

While climbing up out of the ravine where she had been hiding all night long, Ann Clarke spotted a man with a book tucked under his arm. She made an educated guess, in that instant, that could have cost her life. She predicted that a man who read would be opposed to slavery, not in favor of it.

Ann approached the learned-looking man and told him everything. She told him that she was a slave who had escaped from her masters, and supplicated for his help on her way to freedom. With that, her fate was in this stranger's hands.

The woman's confession was fraught with danger. With the Fugitive Slave Act in full effect, the repercussions for runaway slaves as well as those who helped them were severe, if not lethal. Slaves could be returned to their plantations by anyone, not just the slave owner, even if their identities were discerned outside of slave territory. Anyone who encountered a fugitive slave and did not return the missing "property" could face bank-breaking fines. Indeed some sacrificed their land and livelihood to cover the debts of their moral convictions. If a slave was returned to his or her master after running away, it was common knowledge that the slave would face violent lashings, or worse, upon return.

The risk Ann took when guessing that this unfamiliar white man would be sympathetic to her cause was enormous. But the alternatives— remaining a slave or starving in the ravine—were not options. In that moment, he was her only hope.

Ann's hunch was right. The man was a doctor and a staunch abolitionist. When she encountered him, he was on his way home from

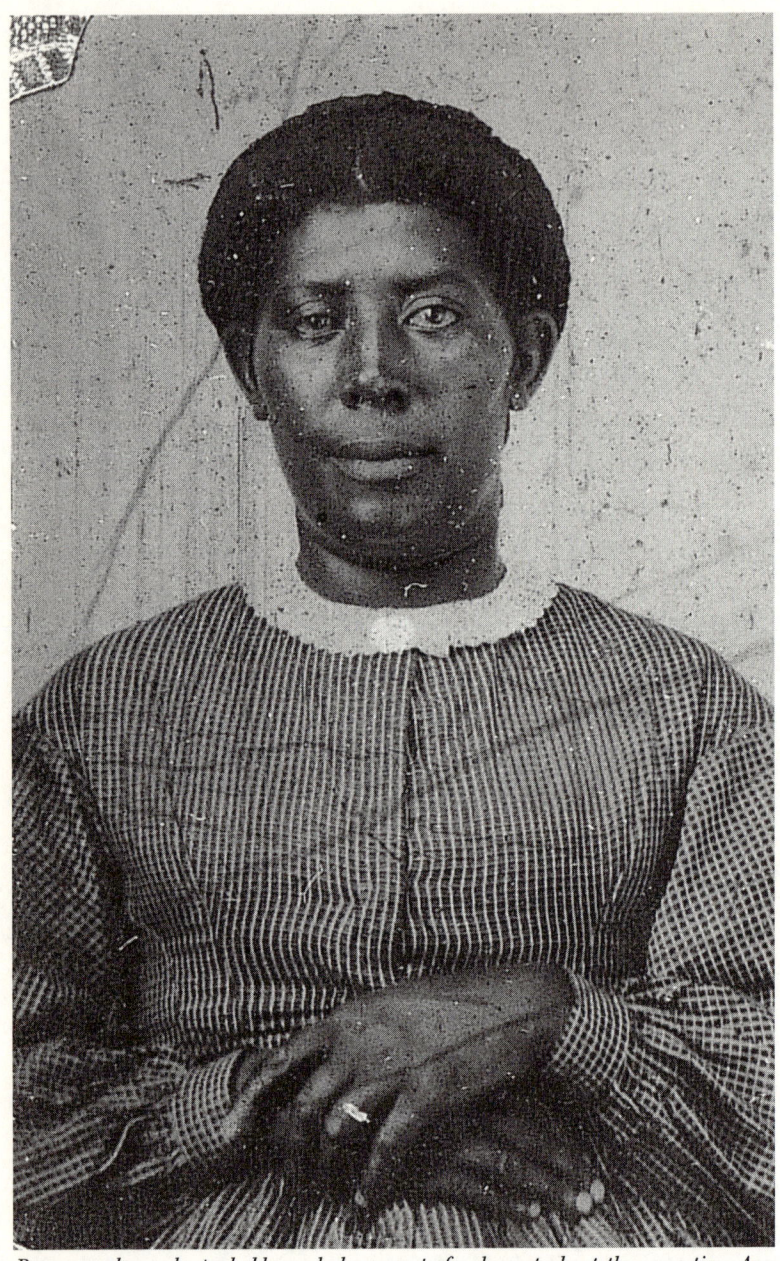

Runaway slave who probably made her way to freedom at about the same time Ann Clarke did Kansas Historical Society

visiting a sick patient. He acted casual as he discreetly spelled out the way to his house, careful not to appear to interact with her, and certainly not taking the risk of accompanying her. Walking together would have put them both in considerable danger. Quietly, out of the side of his mouth, he gave her clear instructions to meet him at a covert back entryway where he would lead her to a hiding place that should be reasonably safe.

There she would stay until he could send her on her way to freedom via the Underground Railroad, an informal network of people who sympathized with the cause of fugitive slaves seeking freedom, and whose houses served as hiding places—or "stations"—along the way. Runaway slaves traveled in hiding from station to station until they reached a place far enough north that they could live without fear of being captured and sent back.

Of course, this is not the beginning of Ann's story, nor is it the end. Where Ann's story begins is hard to say. Birth certificates were not issued when slaves entered the world; often they themselves did not know exactly how old they were, where they were born, or to whom. Their lives were documented as property is documented, not by birth and death, but by sale and transport. They carried the last names of their owners, not their parents.

Ann Clarke was estimated to be about forty-five years old when she ran away from her master in 1857. Her last name, Clarke, came from General W. Clarke of Lecompton, Kansas, who owned her jointly with a neighbor, Colonel Titus.

Compared with other territories, Kansas was home to a very small number of slaves in the 1850s. The first census taken in Kansas in 1855 indicates a total of 242 slaves in the territory. The estimated number of slave owners in Kansas in 1856 was a mere fifty.

In the year of Ann Clarke's great escape, Kansas was at the hot, contentious center of the national debate surrounding slavery. Although eventually admitted to the union as a free state, Kansas was still a mere territory whose admission was delayed by uneasiness surrounding the question of whether new states would permit slavery within their borders. The number of slave states equaled the number of free states, a delicate balance that kept passions on both sides of the issue somewhat contained—but just barely. Although the Missouri Compromise of 1850 dictated that all slaves to the north of the Missouri border be admitted as free states, the Kansas territory was so big that even following the protocol and admitting Kansas as a free state would have ruffled pro-slavery feathers.

It was just a few short years earlier, in 1854, that an Illinois senator proposed a bill that upended the balance, causing Kansas to erupt into violence. When he proposed the Kansas-Nebraska Act, Illinois senator Stephen Douglas (of the now-famed Lincoln-Douglas debates) was not particularly motivated by a keen moral concern for how the slavery debate panned out. He was motivated, rather, by an economic desire to connect Illinois to California by railroad. Obviously, a train going from Illinois to California would need to pass through the sprawling wilderness that stretched from Missouri to New Mexico. The most efficient way to expand the railroad through that territory, as Douglas saw it, was to bring that territory into the Union. The slavery issue perturbed him in that it was holding up the process. His proposed solution was as follows: Split the territory into two states, to be called Kansas and Nebraska. Then let those states have popular sovereignty; that is, allow the residents of those states to vote on whether they would allow slavery within their own borders.

However diplomatic this solution may sound, all hell rapidly broke loose in Kansas as pro- and anti-slavery interests descended upon the state in an attempt to influence the outcome. Meanwhile, President Buchanan had recently established a capital for Kansas Territory: Lecompton, about two miles from where Ann Clarke lived and worked as a slave. Buchanan had a capitol building constructed in Lecompton, and it was in this building—in 1857, just months after

Ann took flight—that the Lecompton Constitution called for Kansas to be admitted as a slave state. Although this document was eventually rejected, Ann Clarke bolted from her owner at what was arguably one of the most dangerous times, and in one of the most conspicuous places, to attempt such a coup.

She initially set out alone, on foot, in early 1857, traveling about twenty miles through the cold, barren plains until she reached Howard's Farm just east of Topeka. There she stayed for about six weeks, waiting for an opportunity to continue heading north. While waiting, however, some pro-slavery men living nearby learned of her whereabouts and descended on Howard's Farm, capturing Ann and hauling her back to Lecompton.

The caravan reached Lecompton in the afternoon. Ann's captors stopped at a hotel to celebrate their triumph, sending a messenger to General Clarke to let him know that they were dutifully returning his runaway slave and requesting their just rewards. While they waited, they drank heavily, leaving Ann to freshen up and eat her lunch in an outdoor kitchen area.

Had Ann been the type to suffer fools gladly, she might have been discouraged by the disappointing turn of events and attempted to regain her master's trust through good behavior, but she hadn't lost all hope for freedom. She noted that her captors had been rendered less vigilant by their drinking and that only the women stood watch over her. She did not eat her lunch. Instead she tucked it away for later, knowing that it might be the only sustenance she would have for some time. Then she watched her captors and waited for her chance to flee. It was wintertime, and darkness descended upon Kansas in the early evening hours, allowing Ann to slip out of her captors' view unnoticed before her master arrived to reclaim her.

She ran to a ravine near the state house in Lecompton. It was dense with brush. She hid all night inside a thicket, not stirring until morning.

The temperature likely hovered near or below freezing. Her captors came out looking for her, and she heard them approach, venturing frighteningly close. But they never did find her in the darkness.

She rose at dawn, climbing out of the ravine to the top of a hill overlooking the expansive, never-ending prairie. She got her bearings and soon encountered Dr. Barker with his legendary, telltale book.

Ann stayed with Dr. Barker for a couple of days before he hitched his team to take her away. She hid beneath comforters in the wagon, remaining well concealed as Dr. Barker drove her to the home of a friend in Lawrence, Kansas, today a well-known college town, but at the time, a Free State stronghold. This friend, in turn, delivered Ann to the home of a Topeka woman by the name of Mrs. Scales.

Mrs. Scales ran a boardinghouse. Typically boarders stayed out of the house during the day and returned for a warm place to sleep at night. So every night during her stay, Ann crawled into the cellar and slept in a large barrel. Her accomplices put some straw, clothes, and blankets into the barrel for her to make her bed warm and soft. During the day, she would help with chores as a way of showing her gratitude.

One day, while Ann was up in the house doing dishes, a pro-slavery boarder named Captain Henry happened to return to the premises unannounced. He saw Ann, but before he could do anything about what he saw before his very eyes, Mrs. Scales said to him, in the form of a command and not a question, "You can keep a secret." Surprisingly, and for unknown reasons, he did.

Ann was delivered to Mrs. Scales's house to meet abolitionist John Armstrong, who not only helped her in the next leg of her journey, but also wrote about Ann's story in his pamphlet titled "Reminiscences of Slave Days in Kansas." Armstrong was not only a pivotal character in the story of how one woman on the lam earned her freedom; he is also the reason we know anything about her story today.

Not many stories of fugitive slaves are as well documented as Ann Clarke's. Many of the Underground Railroad conductors—the people who played important roles in either hiding or transporting runaway slaves—preferred not to ask the escapees where they came from or where they were headed. The less one knew, the easier it was to say "I don't know" under questioning. Most abolitionists wanted to know nothing so as to give away nothing if interrogated by the slaves' pursuers.

Many escapees fled on foot, wandering alone through the woods and in the swamps at night, using the North Star as a compass. Others forged their masters' autographs, presenting fraudulent papers allowing them to travel by train. A number of the fugitives sustained unimaginable levels of personal stress, having left behind spouses and children and usually having survived horrific trauma. Many had been beaten and still bore the bruises. Regardless of the circumstances, however, successful escapes like Ann's didn't usually leave much of a trace, much less a paper trail.

John Armstrong took a keen interest in Ann's story, perhaps because she was the first slave he helped to freedom. What we know about Ann's story, we know only because he documented it. It was Armstrong who assembled everything that would be needed to transport Ann the rest of the way to Chicago: a fleet of mules, for example, and a carriage. Having made a few different stops along the Underground Railroad, Ann and John finally arrived in Civil Bend, Iowa, where John left her with a friend who transported her the rest of the way to Chicago. Ann eventually wrote John Armstrong a letter from Chicago letting him know that she had a daughter living in Missouri. Ann asked John to get her in exchange for five hundred dollars, an even more substantial sum of money in the nineteenth century than now. How Ann went from being a fugitive slave with only one lunch to her name to offering a reward of five hundred dollars for the freedom of her daughter remains a mystery. So, too, does the outcome.

Armstrong doesn't tell us in his reminiscences whether he was able to track down Ann's daughter or not—or whether he tried.

In 1861, just four years after Ann's escape, Kansas was admitted to the Union as a free state, and slavery was outlawed on the land from which Ann fled.

HARVEY GIRLS

— ◆ —

(1877–1968)

INDEPENDENT FRONTIER WOMEN, SERVING MEALS AND SETTLING TOWNS

The path to western settlement was forged in iron. Railroad tracks snaked through the landscape, and where they went, towns and cities followed, first in Kansas, then further west.

But molten iron and calloused, grease-stained hands weren't the only materials needed to settle the West. There were also plenty of lovingly brewed cups of coffee hurriedly served on silver platters, right there beside the railroad tracks.

The coffee was served by hardy women like Olive Winter Loomis, wearing hairnets and starched aprons, working ten-hour days and seven-day weeks, sleeping two or more to a room at night before waking up and doing it again.

Olive grew up on an Arkansas farm. Her parents had been homesteaders in Oklahoma in the 1890s, when droves of families on horseback or in covered wagons hurried to hold down plots of land where they might attempt to turn the red-clay, earthen soil into a fortune. After a few years spent toiling under the hot, unforgiving sun, Olive's parents gave up homesteading in favor of farming in Arkansas. And in Arkansas they stayed.

But Olive still felt restless, as though she hadn't quite found her place in the world. She dreamed of leaving the farm life behind altogether and making a future for herself doing something else, going somewhere else. Having grown up working hard in the fields, however, she didn't have the luxury of a great education that might have prepared her to do anything she wanted. And she certainly wasn't eligible for work on the railroad, as a boy in the same situation would have been. The options for a girl like Olive were limited. And many like her stayed on their family farms not out of a love for farming, but because there didn't seem to be much of a choice.

When Olive heard about a job at a dime store in Topeka, Kansas, she decided it was worth a shot. Compared to her Arkansas farm, Topeka was a big, thriving city. She went for it. She left the farm and was on her way to making her own living.

Unfortunately the job barely lasted a week. Already in Kansas, she turned to the newspaper for leads on other jobs rather than returning home to Mom and Dad—though that's what Mom and Dad would have preferred, and they let her know that in no uncertain terms.

But Olive persisted, determined to make it in Kansas. While scouring the newspaper for jobs, Olive found out about the possibility of working as a Harvey Girl, serving food and drink to weary travelers riding the rails through sparsely populated Kansas.

But what on earth did it mean to be a Harvey Girl?

Well, that's quite a story.

The men who laid railroad tracks struck out in front of the rest of the population, following jobs and setting up temporary, makeshift, ramshackle tent cities that sprung up wherever there was work. They'd pave the way for settlement and then move on to the next seasonal gig: a harvest in one territory, the transport of a livestock to another, or perhaps laying more track further on down the line. And so a classic American folk song was born:

I've been working on the railroad, all the livelong day
I've been working on the railroad, just to pass the time away.

Harvey Girls Kansas Historical Society

The men who ventured west for work tended to be rough-hewn loners, not family men with sisters, wives, or daughters in tow. These men were out looking for adventure and cold, hard cash—not stability and fine china. They had nothing to lose and everything to gain. Progress was slow on the railroad. It happened one mile at a time. Muscles, picks, and shovels were the only tools these men used, and few if any comforts awaited them when the day was done. They confronted frozen prairie sod in the winter and suffocating heat in the summer. Theirs was a hard, dusty reality.

That was the perception anyway.

This is perhaps where the oft-quoted axiom that there were "no ladies west of Dodge City, and no women west of Albuquerque" came from. Until the 1870s or so, the communities that sprung up around railroad jobs were communities made up largely of single men who worked hard, and—as rumor had it—played hard, too. It was a world deemed unfit for the fairer sex.

Travel to small Kansas railroad towns today, and you'll hear people referring to this era of their own past as "the rough 'n' tumble days." They pronounce these words with a knowing chuckle and a proud twinkle in their eyes.

In the 1870s most towns where the trains stopped consisted of no more than one lone shack and a primitive water tank. Back East, fair-sized towns dotted the railroad's path, so a traveler was never cast out from civilization for long during the journey. But when crossing the prairie's wide expanse, all a traveler could hope to find was a boomtown—a temporary city slapped up to accommodate the most utterly basic needs of railroad workers.

Finding food to last the journey was a huge problem. Travelers who dared to eat in depots suffered prairie dog stew and heavy biscuits known as "sinkers" served on dirty tables by crusty-looking servers giving them the stink eye. And that was *if* they were lucky. Most of the time, travelers merely waited to eat. The questionable delicacies they ordered arrived after passengers had already been called back aboard the train, having paid for food they hadn't had the chance to see, let alone eat.

Some passengers carried their own provisions, but in the pre-air-conditioning era, while rambling slowly down the rails through the hot, desolate Middle West, a piece of chicken from home could become rancid and foul-smelling in no time. As Lesley Poling-Kempes, author of *The Harvey Girls*, puts it, "on the average summer day in Kansas, jolting at twenty miles per hour across the humid, dusty prairie . . . those little boxes of homemade goodies could undergo a sudden change of character." A newspaper writer doing a story on train travel joked that the flies wired ahead for their friends to meet them at the stations.

Enter Fred Harvey. His idea was one we might consider simple today, but it was revolutionary in its own time. Fred Harvey approached the Santa Fe Railroad with the idea of opening quality restaurants at designated stops, where he proposed to offer travelers good food, a comfortable dining atmosphere, freshness, cleanliness, and efficient service. Customers would order from the train cars, and the tally would be communicated to the Harvey House staff by a series of train whistles not unlike Morse code. When the passengers got off the train, their meals would come out promptly, and servers would circulate the dining room offering seconds of everything, ensuring that nobody would be forced to return to the provisionless Wild West on an empty stomach. Whatever supplies Harvey Houses could not get transported to them safely by train, they would purchase from local growers—or grow themselves on their very own dairy farms. Harvey Houses offered something new not only in quality but also in consistency. The consistency extended from the coffee to the service.

At first, all Harvey House employees were men. But, as legend has it, the men acted out and got in brawls at night, showing up for work with big old shiners on their faces in the morning—looking very scrappy, indeed. Scrappy was not the atmosphere Harvey Houses were trying to achieve. In the aftermath of such incidents, Harvey fired his waiters and set about recruiting women from back East.

Nobody believed that the kind of "nice girls" Harvey hoped to hire would be interested in working as waitresses, a profession looked down upon as a code word for prostitution. The reality is that it was extremely uncommon for waitresses to also be prostitutes, but people believed that waitresses were prostitutes, and the stigma kept women from pursuing work in restaurants even though it paid better than other professions open to them, like teaching, for example. If the stigma of the word *waitress* didn't turn them off, the reputation of the unrefined West—with its lack of churches and other staples of polite society—would presumably be the nail in the coffin of Harvey's business plan. And yet, when Harvey placed his ads in East Coast and Midwest city newspapers, he got an avalanche of responses.

The ads read, "WANTED: Young women 18–30 years of age, of good character, attractive, and intelligent." Harvey never used the word *waitress*. He called his servers Harvey Girls. They were associated more with his trademark quality and class than with the food-service profession at large, though food-service professionals is exactly what they were. The women who came to work at Harvey Houses found that although waitresses were looked down upon, Harvey Girls were not.

For the first time, there was a way for single, working women to venture west on their own, to explore their options and settle when and where they chose—like so many young men were already doing—without compromising their social respectability. And venture west they did, in droves.

Part of the trick, it should be stated, is that for all the freedom of mobility Harvey Girls were granted, they lived and worked under the extremely watchful eyes of strict managers who monitored the restaurants, and protective housemothers who monitored their dormitories. They signed contracts agreeing not to marry for the duration of their work commitments, which ranged from six months to a year; if they broke these contracts, they forfeited half their pay. Their rigorous work schedules were prohibitive, often consuming twelve hours a day, keeping them busy on their feet then leaving them dead tired when the day was done. Their work costumes were intended to minimize their feminine charms, not to enhance them: They wore starched, loose-fitting, collared black dresses that fell to eight inches above the floor. Their dresses were belted with big white aprons about as shapely as the average tablecloth. They wore opaque black tights and nearly flat black shoes. They wore matching haircuts as well: short, midneck hair parted down the middle and held in place with a hairnet. No makeup was allowed. Housemothers sometimes enforced the no-makeup rule with a damp cloth. Curfews were nonnegotiable, and rules pertaining to gentleman callers were clear: no men in the bedrooms, only on the porches and supervised sitting rooms of the houses. Men could attend weekly dances at the Harvey Houses by invitation only. If a gentleman caller accompanied one of the women to church on Sunday, that was tantamount to an engagement announcement, and the termination of the attached woman's contract would be forthcoming.

As oppressive as these practices may seem to us today, without them, most of the women's families would not have permitted them to pursue the careers they did, especially so far from home without husbands or parents around to protect their safety and virtue.

What did the women get in return? They made $17.50 a month—decent pay for anyone, woman or man, at the time—in addition to room, board, and free train travel for the adventurous among them. The women took pride in their work, developed sisterhood and lifelong friendships with other like-minded women, gained confidence and poise, earned geographic mobility, and saw the country on their own terms. Some women worked only for a few months. Others worked for decades. Although it was uncommon, some Harvey Girls who did a good job and stuck around awhile even advanced to management positions within the company.

The Harvey Girls are the unsung settlers of the West. They were the founding mothers of many towns that grew up along the railroad routes. With the presence of a female population, men increasingly opted not to move on to that next job out there on the horizon, but to stay put in these fledgling towns, start families, and set down permanent roots. So much for no ladies west of Dodge City and no women west of Albuquerque.

∽

The first six Harvey Houses were erected in Kansas. Even after so many others cropped up in Colorado, Arizona, and New Mexico between the 1880s and the end of the nineteenth century, the Harvey House in Florence, Kansas, was the training ground for all Harvey Girls, regardless of where they would eventually be stationed. So Kansas saw more than its fair share of Harvey Girls in the late nineteenth century.

The lives of twentieth-century Harvey Girls are much better documented than the lives of those who worked in Harvey Houses in the nineteenth century, so it is easier to tell the story of Harvey Girls in general than it is to tell the story of any one Harvey Girl in particular. But a few details about a handful of women's particular lives remain accessible.

Minnie O'Neal grew up on a farm in Leavenworth, Kansas. Her father worked for the railroad and was friends with a Harvey House supervisor who tried to recruit her unsuccessfully for a whole year before the family was persuaded to let her go. Her work as a waitress took her all the way to Raton, New Mexico, in 1885; she was only nineteen years old. The railroad reached Raton six years before Minnie did, and by the time she arrived, it had grown to a whopping four hundred people total and become a town made entirely of clapboard surrounded by mountains as far as the eye could see. The inhabitants were miners, boomers, and cowboys. She considered this the "real outback" of America and viewed her job as a great adventure.

Plenty of women came to Kansas from elsewhere to work for the dining halls and hotels in the Harvey system, like young Matilda Legere, who was born in Belgium. She came to Kansas with her parents in 1879. Her father was a homesteader whose original plot of land was near Cedar Point, Kansas. He was among the many who got a second plot in exchange for planting trees. A year after she arrived in the United States, Matilda started working for the Harvey House in Florence, Kansas. At sixteen years old, she was the youngest girl in the house. In fact, it was unusual, though clearly not unheard of, for women under eighteen to be hired. How the young Matilda got the job in spite of her age is unclear.

She was a hard worker and tried to be efficient, but she was so brusque in her movements that when she met Fred Harvey, he told her, "Don't throw the dishes so hard or you'll break them." If Matilda felt too rushed to be delicate with the dishes, it isn't hard to understand. She had about twenty minutes to serve an entire dining room full of travelers a several-course meal, topped off with the coffee that Harvey Houses were known for, all before the trains once again departed. About eight trains passed through town every day, and each carried around fifty passengers, who ate at a total of six tables that had to be set and cleaned and set again between every meal.

Add to that the stringent Harvey House standards, and this was no leisurely service job. Coffee that sat for two hours had to be tossed and brewed anew, and customers who ordered orange juice could expect that their juice would be squeezed fresh, especially for them. If Fred Harvey showed up for one of his infamous unannounced visits and found a pitcher of presqueezed orange juice in the refrigerator, someone could expect to be fired for the transgression. If he found a chipped plate still in circulation, he might well throw it on the floor to make a point. On the unusual occasions when a Harvey House was slow, Harvey Girls polished silver service items. Some former Harvey Girls insisted that when they eventually stocked kitchens of their own, the one thing they never wanted was silver— they had polished enough silver while working in Harvey Houses to last them a lifetime.

A woman who came to the Florence, Kansas, Harvey House at around this same time was a widow from Illinois by the name of Lofgren. Young widows needed to function as breadwinners for entire families, and as a result, they were numerous among Harvey Girls. This particular widow got a little help on the job from one of her daughters, who managed to pick up a few cents of her own here and there. Lofgren also picked up extra work as a Swedish interpreter.

Joanne Thompson was another of the widows who found work in the Harvey Houses of Kansas. She stuck with the business for more than forty years, eventually working as a manager in Topeka, Dodge City, and beyond. In this way, she supported herself and her daughter.

To women who hailed from bustling metropolises, the makeshift town of Florence, Kansas, must have seemed awfully remote, if not completely unhinged from civilization. Even today, when traveling to Florence on the highway by car, this area feels perilously untethered from modern America. Located in the Flint Hills, Florence is a mite of a town. According to a billboard welcoming today's highway travelers to Florence, the town is "nestled in a valley." It's nestled, alright. When you reach the edge of town—and you *will* reach the edge of town if you walk in any cardinal direction for about fifteen minutes—the last street you encounter will butt up against a hill. Florence is not just nestled between two of these massive, low-lying, grassy hills under a bright blue sky. It just barely manages to squish itself to fit into the tiny space between them.

If one must use a restroom or find a cup of coffee or mail a letter in Florence, Kansas, that person will be hard-pressed to find a public place of business where such a transaction might be possible. With a population of around six hundred today—hardly more than in the Harvey House days—the town does not contain a single consistently open storefront business. Sure, there's a bar—called the General Store—open Thursday, Friday, and Saturday nights. There is another store, open seasonally, that sells Christmas trees and other holiday paraphernalia. Members of the American Legion have a private clubhouse on the main street. But the library, post office, and high school in town have all closed their doors. So has a business called Some Where Else!. It may not be entirely clear what sort of commerce happened Some Where Else!, but it is certain that somewhere else is exactly where it went. Although people continue to live in beautiful, well-maintained Victorian houses along the brick and cobblestone roads of Florence, they all commute to work in far-flung locales. Some of them even cross county lines to retrieve their paychecks.

And yet, hearing their own footsteps reverberate on the brick roads in town, visitors might experience a mere fraction of the isolation that would have characterized Florence in the late nineteenth century, accessible only by train, were it not for the Harvey House.

But compared to some of the places the Harvey Girls had previously called home, the Kansas towns they traveled to for work, such as Florence, might have seemed like urban meccas. Johanna Klenke, hailing from a Kansas farm and venturing off to be a Harvey Girl like her three older sisters had done before her, said that "leaving the farm and going to work at Dodge City was as exciting as living in New York City for me."

For rural women who didn't have the luxury of a refined education, being a Harvey Girl was a chance to acquire useful skills, acclimate to city life, and to find a path in life that ventured beyond the family farm. Not only that, but a system was put in place to allow Harvey Girls from farming backgrounds to go home to help their families during the summer, when the work load on midwestern farms required all hands on deck. Management simply replaced the farm girls with teachers wanting to make a little extra money while school was out. When the teachers returned to the classrooms and farm work returned to normal, the Harvey Girls reported back for duty in their dining rooms by the railroad tracks.

∽

The Harvey House in Florence, Kansas—where the Harvey House Museum and Harvey House Historical Society are now based—was established in 1878. Fred Harvey bought an existing hotel, the Clifton Hotel, and set up his dining hall inside it. By 1879, due to increased tourism in the area and therefore increased demand, the Clifton Hotel and Harvey House expanded, becoming one of the largest buildings in central Kansas. In just six months of 1879, the hotel accommodated a total of 2,300 guests.

This was good for the town, and good for area farmers, too. Harvey was notorious for his commitment to quality over cost cutting, and he paid farmers top dollar for the ingredients they grew or produced. The manager at the Florence Harvey House paid unheard-of sums of money for prairie chickens, quail, butter, fruits, and vegetables.

The Harvey House was also home to the first shower in Florence, which might seem strange now that indoor plumbing is commonplace, but at the time—in a boomtown—it was a novelty. The Harvey House didn't have indoor plumbing, either—at least, not in the twenty-first-century sense of those words. There was a tank in the attic that had to be filled with water from the cistern to keep the water supply available for all this showering. And yes, there was a lot of showering. The Harvey House opened the shower to the whole town. For twenty-five cents, anyone could have a rainwater bath—it was open to ladies on Tuesday and Friday, and to men the rest of the week. This was considered a true luxury.

Historians have argued that the Harvey Girls populated and "civilized" the West by marrying the local men and starting families with them, as well as churches and other such symbols of society and its permanence. Thanks to the Harvey Girls, they say that what was once the wild Wild West is now friendly terrain dotted with bungalows and lined with sidewalks. But on a very basic level, the Harvey Girls brought simpler things. They brought amenities like showers. They brought a demand for fresh food and the local agricultural commerce that goes with it. They brought civic pride to the towns that could boast their own Harvey Houses. And they brought themselves: independent-minded, intelligent, hard-working women with the confidence and determination to found fledgling communities. When Fred Harvey placed ads looking for Harvey Girls, people underestimated how many young women were interested in going west and game for the risk and the challenge. The pioneering spirit was alive and well across gender lines.

In Hollywood's 1946 movie *The Harvey Girls*—starring a wide-eyed Judy Garland—a train full of energetic, rosy-cheeked young women heads for a town out West. All of the ladies on the train, except Judy Garland, plan to become Harvey Girls.

The Harvey Girls on Garland's train laugh while lunching on bountiful provisions; Garland herself nibbles on a meager snack.

When the Harvey Girls find a way to give her some food without shaming her, they ask her where she's headed and why. It turns out she has corresponded with a frontiersman after answering a matrimonial ad and has boarded this train to meet her future husband in person.

When her future husband turns out to be a bit of a disappointment, Judy Garland grabs her bags and hightails it to the Harvey House where her fellow passengers are still filing in the front door.

"Well," she announces with a studied pout. "It looks like you just got yourself another Harvey Girl." And the housemother waves her in with the others.

It's not a particularly historically accurate story—to become a Harvey Girl, applicants were thoroughly screened through a selective interview process and a background check. But it does capture the public's romanticized perception that being a Harvey Girl was glamorous. Being a Harvey Girl was hard work, but it was hard work that was admired and respected and did not cast doubt upon a young woman's station in life. Her efforts were regarded without harsh judgment—perhaps because she was invariably pretty.

Countless poems were written in the Harvey Girls' honor. This one was written by John Moore:

> *One crisp December Morn—*
> *Chilly was the day,*
> *I sat behind my coffee*
> *In a Harvey House Cafe.*

Fred's coffee is a nectar—
a beverage supreme,
And the girl who serves it
Adds glamour to my dream. . . .

❧

The aroma most enticing,
Blending with the steam,
The face across the hazy cup—
The vision of a queen.

❧

I like my morning coffee,
Before the busy noon,
When she has time to chatter,
While I dally with my spoon.

❧

All dressed in spotless linen,
Her hair all in a curl,
So purely sweetly winning,
Is the happy Harvey girl.

As for Olive Loomis, who left her home in Arkansas in search of a future beyond her family's farm, she applied for a job as a Harvey Girl, and her application was successful. She got herself a steady job and a place to live in Emporia, Kansas, in no time, and didn't have to limp back home with her tail tucked between her legs.

Although her parents initially disapproved of her chosen line of work, the Harvey House job provided her great financial stability for much of her life. She worked in the Harvey House system for nineteen years.

Her parents presumably got used to the arrangement.

Nora Holt

(1885–1974)

CLASSICAL COMPOSER,
HARLEM RENAISSANCE NOTABLE,
TABLOID SWEETHEART

Nora Holt—born Lena Douglas in Quindaro, Kansas—was a woman of many names and many firsts.

First African American to get her master's degree in music. First woman to write for an African-American newspaper in a major city. She was also a woman of many jobs. She worked as a composer, musician, music critic, music teacher, radio show host, and—for a little while anyway—hair stylist and salon owner. She lived the life of a Renaissance woman. A *Harlem* Renaissance woman. But Harlem was a long way from Nora's home, and this Renaissance woman's story has humble beginnings in a historically significant Kansas township now reduced to crumbling stone rubble, vacant lots, and tumbleweed.

The township of Quindaro—which has all but vanished in recent decades—bloomed almost overnight on the banks of the Missouri River just across the water from the neighboring state of Missouri. The town, whose name means "bundle of sticks" or "in union there is strength," was founded in 1856 by New Englanders who had traveled to Kansas to establish an anti-slavery presence there. With the slave state of Missouri within view and Kansas still a mere territory with its stance on slavery undecided, this is where people came to fight the good fight. Quindaro's identity and existence were based on a desire to change the fate of the country by steering the course of Kansas. It was, most famously, a place of refuge for escaped slaves. When Missouri slaves made it to Quindaro, they could count on finding abolitionists who would move them to safety in the North via the Underground Railroad. Quindaro was the notorious first stop, well-known to pro-slavery forces and runaway slaves alike. It was a dangerous, exciting place to be.

By 1858, the town boasted hundreds of buildings made of stone, standing testament to dreams of permanence. One of the first buildings erected was a fancy hotel, Quindaro House, which kept something strange in the basement: a tunnel that led to the river. The tunnel's original purpose was to conceal the passage of escaped slaves from danger in Missouri to safety in Kansas.

The tunnel under the fancy hotel became a favorite play spot for kids born at the end of the nineteenth century. Kids born after Quindaro's heroic and prosperous "gateway to Kansas" days grew up on stories of people risking their necks for freedom. These kids spent lazy afternoons playing John Brown in the tunnel they proudly believed he built.

The tunnel would later appear in an advertisement for an all-black college that briefly existed in Quindaro, the school from which Nora Holt would graduate as valedictorian in 1915: Western University.

With a population made of fearless, progressive-minded New Englanders who had left their homes to help others find freedom, and escaped slaves who had fled their homes in the cover of night and risked their lives for their own freedom, Quindaro was a forward-thinking, anything-is-possible kind of place. In this setting, a Presbyterian minister by the name of Eben Blachly started a school in his home, teaching the children of escaped slaves how to read and write, both before and during the Civil War. His was one of many homes throughout the Midwest that served this function.

One cold February day in 1865, a group of Quindaro men met to talk about the possibility of building a university. The talk appears to have gone well, as the men marched straight to the courthouse to draw up a formal document for the founding of a school that very same day. The state of Kansas supported the goal of black education by giving all

Nora Holt Photograph by Carl Van Vechten, courtesy of the Van Vechten Trust

the town's land to the new school, essentially forfeiting its claim on taxes from the township.

When Eben Blachly died in 1877, the school quickly deteriorated. It was almost immediately replaced by Western University, built in the model of Booker T. Washington's Tuskegee Institute. In 1883, Western University became an industrial school where black students would learn a profitable trade that they could use to advance in the world after graduation. The first class—consisting of a whopping eight students—graduated in 1898.

At this time, the school had only one building that resembled a church. When the cornerstone was laid for the first Western University building to be erected by the state of Kansas, black and white people alike came to hear Governor Stanley's remarks. The year was 1900.

"The colored man needs no more than the white man to make success easy," he said. "All that either wants is opportunity." Although Governor Stanley did not mention what a woman of either race might need for success, Nora Holt found it at Western University more than a decade later.

By the time Nora Holt (then Lena Douglas) came to Western University, the campus had grown from one building to eight, and it now included a Girls' Trades building—which housed the music studio. The music department was started in 1902 with just three pianos, one reed organ, an orchestra, a twenty-two-piece brass band, and one lone teacher. The department was so popular, however, that by 1910, three pianos had grown to ten, and one teacher had increased to three instructors. Students in the music department were required to practice their instrument of choice two and a half hours a day. The department offered a rigorous, four-year program in theory, harmony, analysis, piano, voice, orchestra, and marching band.

By now, the founder of the music department had also started a group of a cappella jubilee singers who became well-known throughout the United States. In addition to singing on campus and in town, they made radio appearances and traveled to thirty-nine states for shows. It was in the Jackson Jubilee Singers that Western University valedictorian Lena Douglas (later known as Nora Holt) got her start as a performer. She also wrote the school's official song, "O Western University."

Of course, she arrived at Western already versed in music. Her mother, Grace Brown Douglas (or Gracie, as she was known), and her father—a Methodist minister by the name of Calvin Douglas—signed her up for piano lessons when she was only four years old. She showed promise from the get-go. One of her teachers, N. Clark Smith, noticed her talent and took her to symphony concerts. Having caught the attention of N. Clark Smith puts Nora in good company; he taught some of the finest musicians to emerge from the gritty Kansas City scene.

Most Western University students didn't get to fraternize much with the musicians in downtown Kansas City. Western's campus was tucked away in the woods of Quindaro. According to scholars, the school was deliberately hidden for the purpose of keeping the students on campus and out of trouble. The fear was that if the students had better access to the nightlife in the city, they might rub elbows with the wrong crowd and get in trouble with the bottle or the law.

Fresh out of proud Quindaro, having risen to the very top of her graduating class, Lena was not content to rest on her laurels. She didn't stick around. Instead she flew the coop, taking advantage of her freedom and her musical education in a place where opportunities for musicians abounded. Off she went to Chicago, where she continued her formal study of music in graduate school and became the first African American to earn a master's in music, paying her way through school by singing and playing the piano to provide live entertainment for the crème de la crème at parties thrown by the elite families of Chicago in the most stylish apartments. Composition was her forte, and for her master's thesis, she composed a symphonic rhapsody for strings. The classical composition was based on a black spiritual called "You May Bury Me in the East."

The lyrics to the song are about the irrepressible nature of an ascendant soul:

You may bury me in the East / You may bury me in the West / But I'll hear that trumpet sound / In the morning . . . In that dreadful judgment day / We'll take wings and fly away / But I'll hear that trumpet sound / In the morning.

Nora believed that to preserve this song and other spirituals for future generations, it was important to bring them to life through dignified classical composition and performance, to introduce a musical genre that had always been respected, and always would be. (Unfortunately, her compositions have largely been lost to time as they were stolen while she was touring in Europe and Asia in the 1930s.)

The only Nora Holt composition to survive is a piece called "Negro Dances," a cascading ragtime piece for piano that has been said to rival anything written by celebrated ragtime composer Scott Joplin. The song is included on ragtime compilation CDs and is even available online for anyone who would like to hear it.

While preparing for her master's degree, Nora began to take an increasing interest in music criticism. At the same time, her zeal for performing as a musician and composing her own songs began to diminish. She began writing as a music critic for an African-American newspaper called the *Chicago Defender* in 1917, a year before she finished graduate school. Her first article appeared on the Women's Page.

Women were still newcomers to journalism, and African-American women in particular had yet to truly break into the field when Nora began writing for the *Defender*. In 1917, she was the only woman writing for a major black newspaper in the United States. With respect to both race and gender, she felt that she was taking on an important responsibility. Her mission was to encourage and entitle readers in the black community to get out and explore the arts, to consume and enjoy the bounty of highbrow culture that the city had to offer. She also wanted to help young black artists and seasoned black artists alike gain recognition and flourish in their careers. But she had absolutely no interest in promoting music that wasn't truly worthwhile. She wasn't just trying to make the case for black musicians after all; she was also trying to make a case for herself.

She knew that it was important to earn her readers' trust, to show that she was an expert in her field and that she was a credible music critic and scholar with the gift of discernment. It was important to her that her reviews be taken seriously. Her taste was informed, and it mattered to her that her readership knew that. This mattered to her so much that she refused, early in her career, to accept jazz as a legitimate art form, clinging to the notion that classical music was the highest aspiration for any musician or composer of any race to pursue. It should be noted that this position earned her a reputation as a bit of a snob.

In March 1919, Nora invited a group of Chicago musicians to her home to talk about starting a formal network of black musicians. Her reasoning was that having a formal network would make it easier for young hopeful musicians to exchange encouragement, support, and information—and for established musicians to offer much-needed guidance, inspiration, and opportunity to those following in their footsteps. It was in Nora's home that the National Association of Negro Musicians was born. The group that formed in March was strictly a Chicago organization, but when news of a possible national organization out of Washington, DC, surfaced, Nora took matters into her own hands and convinced the group in Washington to build on what she had already started in a city with a lot of active black musicians, rather than beginning again from scratch outside the thick of it.

In 1919, a five-dollar membership fee to the National Association of Negro Musicians got a young performer the following: the chance to meet and compare notes with musicians who lived in other cities; the chance to hear concerts; the chance to learn the newest teaching techniques in music education; the chance to discuss shared problems and come up with solutions together; the chance to be heard by peers and to meet renowned artists; and the chance to perform at the annual national convention, where members of church choirs from around the country could find themselves singing alongside some of the biggest names in entertainment at the time.

The National Association of Negro Musicians still exists today, and continues to provide vital support to young black musicians. The mission of the organization hasn't changed in spirit since Nora Holt started it. "The National Association of Negro Musicians," reads the mission statement, "promotes, preserves, and supports all genres of music created or performed by African Americans."

Nora believed, and wrote in the *Chicago Defender* in 1918, that "music is one of the greatest refiners of the Race." What she meant by that, exactly, is hard to say. The idea that a race should need to refine itself might seem dated today, but we hear echoes of this notion in current debates about the validity of art forms like rap music and hip-hop, genres that represent pride and accomplishment for the black community according to some, and shame and degradation according to others. The notion that the kind of music a group of people listens to and performs somehow reflects upon that group's human dignity is one that is revisited in some form or another in every generation.

It would seem, however, that Nora was mostly attempting to encourage her African-American readers to feel entitled not only to sing the songs and play the instruments, but also to enjoy music, to listen and dance and talk about it the next day. She maintained her integrity as a music critic for a largely black readership even when she rejected jazz, had a publicly disastrous personal life, and maintained a performance schedule of her own that consisted almost entirely of singing and playing the piano at private parties rather than in concert halls. This dedication to the pursuit of reviewing black music for black audiences speaks volumes of the importance she placed on getting the word out—and not just to well-heeled white patrons of the arts.

During her lifetime, tragically, Nora was best known to those outside her readership as a party girl with a tendency to marry and divorce with great regularity and fanfare—not as a scholar, composer, and musician. When she married George Holt, a wealthy hotel baron many years her senior, rumors circulated as to the true nature of her intentions. When she later married Joseph Ray—the right-hand man to steel magnate Charles Schwab—her motives, again, came into question. The press published nasty, speculative things about her. *Ebony* magazine even gave her the dubious title of "Most Married Negro."

Nora, however, never stooped to their level. She rose above the riffraff.

When her divorce from Joseph Ray made headlines in 1926, provoking even more gossip than the wedding had incited just nineteen months earlier, she told the *Chicago Defender,* "I have never, to any person or newspaper, made any statement against Mr. Ray and there is plenty I could and may have to say, but I maintain that only crude and uncultured people fight out their domestic differences in public." This came after accusations of adultery, fraud, and an endless series of suits and countersuits that kept her name in the newspapers whether she spoke to reporters or not. To her, it was never her own integrity that was in doubt, it was only her reputation that the ordeal threatened. In a letter to a friend, she wrote, "The whole thing is a flimsy suit, no weight and I can beat it hands down, but did not want the annoyance."

Nora's unconventional ways were not such a problem for her in Harlem, where she became a well-known and beloved figure in the Harlem Renaissance. A racy song she used to sing—"My Daddy Rocks Me with One Steady Roll"—became her signature tune, as well as the basis for "Rock Around the Clock," though the latter had much tamer lyrics. Many of her closest friends were writers in the Harlem scene: Langston Hughes, for example, and the controversial Carl Van Vechten, who based an enchanting seductress in one of his novels on Nora's enchanting beauty, magnificent talents, and beguiling ways. Of the character, Lasca Sartoris, he wrote, "It could hardly be said that Harlem, generally speaking, had received the tidings of Lasca's wayward adventures with approval, even equanimity, but those who knew her . . . liked her."

After many years touring and performing in Europe and Asia, Nora lived in both New York and California. During her stint in Los Angeles, she opened a salon and worked as a music teacher in the California school system before finding her way back to New York in 1944, to accept the post of music critic first for the *Amsterdam News*, and later for the *New York Courier*.

She made her mark in the field of broadcast journalism as well, starting the annual *American Negro Artists* festival on radio station WNYC in 1945. From 1953 to 1964, she served as producer and musical director for a weekly radio show for WLIB in Harlem. Nora's show, called *Concert Showcase,* brought the sounds of up-and-coming black musicians to radio listeners all over New York City. It functioned as a true platform for black musicians and composers, influencing the tastes of generations to come and encouraging countless black musicians to keep writing and performing their music, knowing that there was an outlet for it.

In the end, the fame and recognition she earned was not for herself, as she has been mostly forgotten since her time, but for the younger black musicians whose work she covered and whose dreams she encouraged.

And what about her ties to her home state of Kansas? Perhaps it is fitting that Nora Lena Douglas James Scroggins Holt Ray never laid down roots in her western home. It was a home that gave her a music education, freedom, and wings to fly away and make something of herself, just like the spiritual she transformed into a timeless classical composition instructed.

"We'll take wings and fly away," the song goes. "But I'll hear that trumpet sound in the morning."

Nora Holt made good on those words.

ELLA DELORIA

(1888–1971)
SIOUX ANTHROPOLOGIST, TEACHER, AND NOVELIST

In the Sioux Indian territory of South Dakota, a huge gray rock mysteriously shoots up out of the ground. You cannot miss it. The towering basalt structure with deep, vertical grooves etched into its surface is a well-known landmark in the area.

The white men call it Devil's Tower, but that isn't what the Indians call it, because the Indian religions have no such thing as a devil. The Indians call it Bear Rock. According to a Sioux folktale, the vertical lines are the furious scratch marks of a hungry bear.

The story begins something like this: Two little boys were playing with a ball, and when the ball flew out into the sagebrush, they followed it out of the village. They heard the rustlings of an animal, and followed the animal to a stream. Then they saw a herd of antelope, and followed the antelope even further from the village. When they got hungry and it was time to go home, the two boys looked around and were startled to discover that they did not know where they were. They began walking in the direction that they believed "home" was, all the while walking further and further away. . . .

$\backsim$

This is, in some way, how Ella Deloria's story begins as well. Though her story eventually takes her to Lawrence, Kansas, Ella Deloria was born to the Sioux tribe of South Dakota—to whom the story of Bear Rock belongs. The two boys who started walking away from the village, in Ella's story, were her father and her grandfather.

Ella Deloria Dakota Indian Foundation

Ella's grandfather Sawse was a medicine man who had a vision that four generations of his family's men first adapted to the white settlers' ways for survival but then came back to once again find themselves grounded in Indian traditions once all danger had passed. Part of this vision was that he would pass along stories of his people to his son, who would pass them to his grandson, who would pass them to his great-grandson and so on. That way, no matter how far the Deloria family wandered from the old ways, they would know them, preserve them, and eventually, when it was safe, return to them.

Sawse anticipated the permanent occupation of Sioux lands and advised his son Philip to embrace the new ways. He set the example by resigning from his post as chief of his band of the Sioux tribe—the Yankton—and taking up farming. He also chopped down trees and sold wood to the settlers traveling along the Missouri River by steamboat.

Having spent his earliest years visiting the sick with his medicine man father, these memories forever etched in his mind, the young Philip attended boarding schools and returned to the Yankton Indian Reservation as a Christian missionary. He married and had a son, but his wife and son both died—first his wife, of influenza, and then his son, of tuberculosis. The grief-stricken but resilient Philip eventually remarried. His second wife gave birth to two daughters and a son. But the wife and son, unbelievably, died like those who came before them. This time Philip grew despondent. He also despaired because his father's vision was increasingly imperiled by the absence of a third generation of sons who could do their part to fulfill it. Philip almost did not recover from his anxiety and grief. He was completely overwhelmed by doubts about his faith, his future, his legacy, and his decision to follow the white settlers' religion and way of life. But finally, he pulled himself together. And again, he married.

His third wife, Mary, already had two daughters when she and Philip met. But Philip and Mary had a child of their own as well. Born during a frightful blizzard in 1889, her English name was Ella Deloria. Her Sioux name, Anpetu Waste Win, meant Beautiful Day Woman. And it surely wasn't the weather that made the day beautiful.

On the occasion of Ella's birth, Philip decided he was done waiting for a son to whom he could pass along the stories of his father and his tribe. He treated Ella as though she were that son, entrusting his legacy to her with utmost confidence. Perhaps this was why that treacherously snowy day was so beautiful to him.

Ella was treated like a son in every sense, even though Philip and Mary did eventually have sons, as well as another daughter. It was Ella who inherited the stories, who met the elders firsthand, and who drove teams of horses with her father, one time resulting in an accident that caused the horses to go wild, the wagon to tumble, and Ella to lose her thumb. As the family heir, she was trusted to do everything and spared nothing.

Although she was a missionary's daughter, she was raised with one foot planted firmly in each world: the white settler's world, and the native, indigenous world. Her upbringing on the Standing Rock Indian Reservation gave her a special perspective and an ability to understand both cultures equally.

Ella spoke all three dialects of the Sioux language, which gave her an advantage over most white anthropologists and ethnographers, whose ranks she joined when her formal studies took her to Columbia University in New York City. Although she was officially studying to become a teacher, it was at Columbia that she met famed anthropologist Franz Boas. Although the white scholar's openness to the possibility that the American Indian was just as intelligent as the European settler who displaced him might strike today's reader as both obvious and tame, it was something of a mind-blowing assertion at the time— and one that resonated, with particular emotional force, in the heart and mind of one Ella Deloria.

At the turn of the century, it was generally believed that if the Indians had been capable of it, they would have developed the very machinery and other trappings of "civilization" that the white man had developed in Europe; the fact that they had not was routinely trotted out as proof of their inherent inferiority. Franz Boas was revolutionary in his suggestion that there might be other explanations for the differences in the paths that these separate civilizations had followed.

In her own book, *Speaking of Indians*, Ella Deloria quotes Franz Boas enthusiastically. In particular, she draws her readers' attention to the following notion:

> *We must bear in mind that none of these [ancient civilizations] was the product of the genius of a single people. Ideas and inventions were carried from one to the other. . . . As all races have worked together in the development of civilization, we must bow to the genius of all, whatever group of mankind they may represent.*

Returning to her own argument, she comes back from this quote with an unusually eager affirmation of Boas's words. "How true!" Ella writes. She adds that, having developed in isolation from other cultures for so long, with needs that differed greatly from the needs of the European, the Native American tribes had invented the things *they* needed—as opposed to all kinds of things that may have seemed crucial to Europeans, but which they themselves did *not* need.

"Imagination and inventiveness are common human potentialities," she argues. "All people invent." She goes on to explain to her readers that it was the Indian who had learned to cultivate corn by the mid-fifteenth century and taught this to the white settler. She also hints that Indian culture did not continue to progress at the same rate after the mid-fifteenth century in large part due to the abrupt disruption of daily life that occurred with the arrival of those very settlers.

"Knowledge of the cultivation of corn, beans, squashes, and other crops had reached most of the tribes," she explains. "Even the most mobile of them had learned to grow corn. Do we realize that these agricultural products were developed by the Indians? From a wild plant with a tiny ear came maize; from a species of the wild cucumber vine came squashes and pumpkins; and so on. . . . They had their own aims and their own methods for achieving them; and those aims and methods were the direct outgrowth of their peculiar situation and life circumstances. They differed in their habits and outlook simply because they were not exposed to the influences of outside cultures. Otherwise, they were just some more of earth's peoples climbing."

Ella's parents did end up having three more children after Ella, and her bond with her younger sister Susan would dramatically reroute the course of Ella's life. At around the time when Ella was finishing up her studies at Columbia, her mother died, and Susan started having serious health problems stemming—the family would later learn—from several benign brain tumors, which would have to be removed.

At a time when she might otherwise have been furthering her career, Ella found herself instead tending to her sister. She took Susan with her to Lawrence, Kansas, and got a job teaching at Haskell Indian School. She taught physical education and drama—both totally unrelated to her area of specialization—and stood out among teachers there, the majority of whom were white. The Indian students she taught eventually grew up to appreciate her sensitivity to their predicament as they left their tribes and families behind and not only learned but also assimilated.

As Paul Boyer wrote in a special report on Native American colleges prepared for the Carnegie Foundation in 1997, "From the times of the first English settlement, Native Americans have been encouraged to participate in this ritual of Western Civilization. But the goal was almost always assimilation, seldom the enhancement of Indian students or the well-being of their tribes."

Haskell was no exception. Students were not allowed to go home to their families for three full years after arriving, because that would set the school back in its efforts to condition the young people to live in the manner of whites. In the school's records, letters from a mother begging the school to let her children come home to see their dying father one last time appear to have gone unanswered. The cemetery includes heart-wrenching grave plots etched with the names "Somebody's Brother" and "Somebody's Sister."

Ella Deloria's role as a teacher was much more about who she was than the subject she taught. One former student says of Ella Deloria and the other native teacher, Ruth Muskrat Bronson, "They taught their students to have healthy respect for themselves as individuals and a pride in their heritage. They taught us about Indian values and kept them alive in us. . . . They taught us that we could accomplish anything we set our minds to. . . . They taught us how to defend ourselves, as Indian people, without getting angry or defensive."

Ella wrote pageants—that is, educational plays about Indian culture—for her students to perform at white churches and schools. For most of her students, this was a rare opportunity to dispel myths about themselves and to express pride in their heritage in an era when ethnic pride and cultur-ally sensitive approaches to teaching were foreign concepts in mainstream America. Her students would recall the excursions as "expressions of our Indianness that may not otherwise have been possible, given the poverty and discrimination so prevalent on most reservations." At the same time, she was also taking care to familiarize her students with social environ-ments outside their own tight-knit communities, hoping to prepare them to survive wherever their lives might take them.

Throughout her tenure as a teacher in Lawrence, Ella maintained contact with Franz Boas, continuing to work for him doing ethno-graphic research on Indian tribes on the side as much as her teaching schedule would allow. When physical education facilities at the school were under construction, for example, Ella cranked out reports to Boas, who paid her per report. But she could never earn enough money to support herself and Susan—who required brain surgery—if she allowed herself the time it would take to fully dedicate herself to studying the culture, language, and traditions of the Dakota Sioux.

In a letter she wrote to Dr. Boas in 1926 that accompanied her writing, Ella tried to explain to her mentor—who had evidently asked her whether she might be available to lecture on the Sioux Indians—that the need for money was all that stood in her way.

"My sister has had to defer her operation, until I can get the necessary amount of money together. . . . I wish somehow it were possible for me to leave here, and take her with me to do this type of work, but I realize how it is difficult to raise money for such things. . . . I know I can do it, but it is the need for a steady income that I can bank on while I am getting myself known, that is holding me back."

Meanwhile, the research Ella was doing whenever she possibly could was truly groundbreaking. Being Indian herself and fluent in Indian languages, Ella had access to information that was far beyond the reach of her colleagues. When Indian women discussed their problems among themselves, Ella was there to listen to and record their conversations. But native women did not consider it proper to air concerns to men, or to outsiders, and so their fears and dissatisfactions could only be learned through another native woman. As such, the Office of Indian Affairs sent her to South Dakota in 1936 to attend a meeting between Washington officials and native women, where the women would learn about the proposed Reorganization Act, which sought to reorganize tribal lands, expand freedom of religion, and allow tribal self-government. The women themselves had requested the meeting out of concern for future generations.

Those who attended were not, as Ella had imagined, young women with European-style educations who would be well versed in national politics, but in fact they were older women with very little, if any, formal education. Because Ella could understand both what the women said during the official proceedings, in English, and what they said to one another off the record, in Dakota, she was able to shed light on their fears and frustrations. One woman hoped that the land would be reorganized, for example, because presently the land that she had fenced in, plowed, and sown to grain was serving not as fertile farmland, but as a refuge for grasshoppers who hid there from the hooves of white men's cattle, who stampeded the leased Indian lands surrounding her plot. "I am doing very well at pasturing grasshoppers for white ranchers," Ella transcribed in her notes, "instead of raising grain to feed my family!"

While listening to these women, Ella secretly wished that she could stay and continue learning of their lives, their desires, and their fears.

When Franz Boas asked her to teach American Indian dialects to anthropology students at Columbia University, Ella was finally able to quit teaching at Haskell and to travel to reservations for research, interview elders, and publish scholarly works on her findings. She wrote three major works: *Dakota Texts,* documenting myths and stories; *Dakota Grammar,* which is a guide to the Dakota language; and *Speaking of Indians,* which sheds light on the day-to-day life and culture of the Dakota people. In *Speaking of Indians,* Ella explains everything from how quarreling members of a tribe resolve their conflicts to how families merge on the occasion of marriage, to the relationship between how Dakota people address one another and how they address God in prayer.

Her most lyrical work, a tenderly written novel called *Waterlily,* was not published until 1988. It is the story of a family and a tribe, told from the perspective of many generations of women: the grandmotherly Gloku, her daughter-in-law Blue Bird, and Blue Bird's daughter, Waterlily.

But the character who perhaps most resembles Ella Deloria herself in this novel is not any of these women, but a man by the name of

Woyaka, the tribe's prized storyteller. Remember that Ella's grandfather had a plan and a vision to be carried out by future generations of sons. Remember, too, that her elders decided to treat Ella as a son to whom they could pass along stories that could bring the old ways back to life long after they had disappeared.

In *Waterlily*, when explaining to a crowd of spellbound children how he became a teller of tales, the fictional Woyaka says to them:

Regard me, my grandchildren, and observe that I am very old. I have passed more than eighty winters. Many a man of lesser years finds his eyesight fading, his hearing gone, his memory faulty, while I retain my powers and remember everything I hear. That is because my grandfather had a plan for me, and never rested in carrying it out. The day I was born he looked on me and vowed to make me the best teller of stories that ever lived among the Tetons. And to that end he never gave up training me. . . . "Now tell me," he would say, "what was that you heard last night?" And woe to me if I could not give it step by step without a flaw! Gravely, he would then tell me, "Grandson, speech is holy; it was not intended to be set free only to be wasted. It is for hearing and remembering." . . . Did other boys find life easy? Could they daydream all they liked and fritter their time away? Then it was because their elders had no plan for them. My grandfather had a plan for me and that was why he had to be stern—to carry it out. In truth, I was his very heart, and he was a kind man by nature. But he wanted me to be a storyteller, and he spared no means to make me one. "You owe it to our people," he would say. "If you fail them, there may be nobody else to remind them of their tribal history."

Maybe this character was pure fiction. But his story sure sounds an awful lot like Ella's. Only in her case, to tell the story of her own tribe, she had to go very far from home in order to return. To New York, to Kansas, and through periods of extreme poverty. All to bring the world the stories of the people who were her home.

Which brings us back to the boys in the Dakota tale at the beginning of the chapter. In trying to get home, they kept traveling further and further away.

They wished that their elders would find them and take them home. They hoped to see their mother or father, their aunts or their uncles, but none of these comforting, familiar faces appeared. Instead, a big bear found them and chased them, and though they ran as fast as they could, they still could not outrun him. Just as they were about to be eaten for sure, the ground shook and a rock emerged beneath them, raising them up off the ground, carrying them safely out of reach of the growling, slobbering, ferociously hungry bear. The bear clawed at the rock and clawed at the rock and kept clawing at the rock, trying to climb it, but he couldn't. And finally he got tired and wandered off, leaving only the marks of his claws.

According to legend, nobody knows how the boys got down and found their way home. Nobody has proof that they did make it home, but members of the Dakota tribe do have faith in the boys' survival. As the elder who told the story to visiting ethnographers said, "We can be sure that the Great Spirit didn't save those boys only to let them perish of hunger and thirst on top of the rock."

And Ella Deloria didn't suffer for naught; she lived a tough life and died poor and under-recognized, but because of her, the Dakota language survives on the printed page, and her people's stories and customs remain safely preserved for generations to come.

PEGGY HULL

(1889–1967)

FOREIGN WAR CORRESPONDENT,
SOLDIERING THROUGH ADVERSITY

Plenty of reasonable human beings have lived entire lives governed by these prudent words of wisdom: Better safe than sorry. But intrepid World War I reporter Peggy Hull always suspected there was more to life than playing it safe.

It's not just that the young journalist from Kansas reported on the lives of American soldiers from within earshot of gunfire—though she did. It's how she got to the battlefield in the first place that reveals her true grit. The battles she waged and risks she took on her way to the front line required at least as much courage as the job she was expected to do once she got there.

Throughout her career, she followed opportunity from city to city and state to state, letting go of what was certain and secure in favor of what held promise and possibility, unwavering in her confidence that, even when the odds were against her, her talent and determination would pay off. And they did.

Peggy had more in common with the soldiers she covered than with her fellow correspondents. "I did not go to war because I liked the excitement or what my colleagues would sometimes erroneously refer to as the glamour," she would later say. "I went because I was not a man and could not carry a gun and do something for my country." Peggy Hull could turn a phrase to win the hearts and minds of even the most hardened readers. But first and foremost, she was a fighter, and to her, the pen was a weapon.

She had to fight for survival from a young age. Peggy was born Henrietta Eleanor Goodnough on a farm just a few miles outside of

Peggy Hull Peggy Hull Collection, Kansas Collection at the Spencer Research Library, University of Kansas

Bennington, Kansas, in 1889, and her childhood offered very little in the way of security and stability. When she was five years old, her parents divorced, and the split was fraught with drama. Her father accused her mother of having an affair, neglecting her domestic responsibilities, and being unfit for parenthood. Her mother accused her father of failing to provide sufficient financial support, and of neglect and cruelty. She claimed to have married her husband when she was too young to know what love was, and she refused to uphold wedding vows made when she was too young to understand them. The court granted the couple a divorce, which was uncommon in those days.

But the spectacle did not end there; Henrietta's father demanded custody of his children, pointing to an incident that happened when Henrietta was a baby to support his claim that her mother, Minnie, could not be trusted with the safety and well-being of her own children. While Henrietta, her older brother Edward, and their mother were all traveling together by horse and buggy, they traversed an uneven Kansas field, and Edward fell out of the buggy. Once on the ground, he was then run over by the buggy's rear wheel. He lay unconscious in the field for quite some time, and when he came to, he was all alone. His arrival home was the first signal to his mother that he had been missing in the first place. From that moment on, the shy little Edward stuttered.

The judge devised a compromise regarding the Goodnoughs' custody battle: Edward would stay with his father, and Henrietta would go with her mother. But Henrietta missed her father, and she missed her brother. Furthermore, townspeople shunned her mother, and shunned Henrietta along with her.

The family was happy to pick up and move from Bennington to Marysville and make a new start, the first of many new starts in Henrietta's young life. Her mother and grandmother ran a boardinghouse in Marysville for a while, but when Minnie fell in love and married a housepainter, she and Henrietta moved in with him. Minnie and her husband moved around Kansas and Colorado several times, sometimes taking Henrietta with them and sometimes leaving her with relatives. By the time Henrietta was in high school, her mother and stepfather had finally resettled with some success in Bennington, where Henrietta got to know her brother again. She came into her own, playing the mandolin and becoming the star of the town's very first girls' basketball team. But instability had interrupted her education so many times that in spite of being a studious girl who loved to read, Henrietta did not graduate from high school. The town gossips tsk-tsked, agreeing that it was a pity the girl was allowed to run wild. Henrietta grew up eager for an opportunity to prove them all wrong and to show that it was not such a pity after all.

A voracious reader, the budding young writer favored works by a female journalist named Nellie Bly, whose stunts are considered forerunners of modern-day investigative reporting. Bly did things like trying to go around the world faster than the main character of Jules Verne's *Around the World in Eighty Days*, and faking a nervous breakdown to get herself committed to a mental institution, from whence she could report firsthand on the conditions patients endured inside.

Bly's writing inspired the adventurous Henrietta, who, now unhappily studying pharmacology with expectations of working in a drugstore, quickly sent off job inquiries to Kansas newspapers. She heard back from an editor in Junction City, Kansas, who claimed to have all the reporters he needed, but he could use a typist—if she wasn't afraid of messing up her fingernails, of course.

That was all the encouragement Henrietta required. She was determined to work her way up to writing and reporting in addition to typing. With hope as her only cargo, off she went. To supplement her meager newspaper wages, she worked odd shifts at a department store on the side.

Her family, it should be noted, did not approve of her foray into journalism. Working for a newspaper was considered lowly and crass in those days, especially for a woman. But coming as it did from a family whose reputation could hardly get much worse, this disapproval did not register as worthy of serious consideration. Henrietta loved the crazy intensity of newsroom, calling the atmosphere "part monastery, part abattoir." Eventually, as she predicted, she was writing her own stories, not just typing other people's.

Throughout her early career she advanced by moving eagerly from newspaper to newspaper, an approach that took her all over the United States: Colorado, Hawaii, California, Minnesota, and Ohio are among the states where she resided, making a name for herself almost everywhere she went. Although she did have a short-lived, ill-fated marriage along the way, for the most part, she was single. Her need to support herself financially led her to come up with a variety of clever business ideas, such as offering her readers a personal shopping service called "Let Peggy Shop for You."

It was in Ohio that many important pieces finally fell into place for this struggling writer. First, her editor insisted that Henrietta Eleanor Goodnough was much too unwieldy for a newspaper byline; her first assignment was to come up with something punchier. And so she became Peggy Hull, which turned out to be a great career move.

Second, she came up with an idea for a column that gave her name recognition—and paid her bills, which were substantial as she now lived out of a trunk in a hotel. The scheme: She produced semifictional, semifactual advertising stories about her life in Cleveland. The stories were written in the style of one friend confiding in another. In the course of her stories, she would stumble into high-end retail stores in town and always managed to find exactly what she needed. In a storm she might find a great umbrella, for example. The stores were paid advertisers, and Peggy ran a disclaimer alongside the column making sure readers understood that the proprietors of those shops named in her column had paid for the mention.

Her basic strategy, as she put it, was to make things happen to her. And that is how a third all-important piece of the big puzzle fell into place in Cleveland. One of the things that conveniently happened to Peggy in her column began what would turn into an obsession with military life and war reporting. Peggy joined the Women's Auxiliary of the Ohio National Guard's training school.

Cleveland, it just so happened, was the first city in the nation to establish a National Guard training course for citizens. The idea behind it, at least on the surface, was to prepare civilians for any possible emergency. But in retrospect, it is clear that this was a training ground for the troops who would eventually serve overseas in World War I—a war in which America was not yet involved but soon would be.

Although women could not enlist as soldiers in World War I, they were invited to join the Women's Auxiliary of the National Guard. Peggy didn't miss a beat. She signed up almost immediately. Reporting the news to her readers, she was ecstatic. Her words leapt off the page, as though adrenaline could manifest itself in type.

"I'm a soldier now!" she wrote in the *Cleveland Plain Dealer*. "I'm going to learn to shoot a rifle and do Red Cross work. . . . The drills and exercises are splendid from a health standpoint and the military training teaches self-control, a good thing for the majority of us."

When the Ohio National Guard was called to the Mexican border to search for Pancho Villa, the Women's Auxiliary did not participate in the effort, but Peggy wanted desperately to go and pleaded with her editor to send her as a correspondent. But he wouldn't dream of sending a woman to an army camp, even if she did want very badly to go.

This prompted her to make a bold career move, one that set the precedent for her future dealings with skeptical editors who did not take her ambitions seriously. Although she had a good job, a job she very much needed, she announced to her boss that if he wouldn't send her to the border to cover the Ohio National Guard, she would go anyway. She would write articles keeping people abreast of what was happening. If he didn't want them, she would sell them to any paper that would take them—perhaps even a competitor. Her boldness was rewarded: Her editor reluctantly agreed to buy the articles, but Peggy would have to fund her own voyage because he still wasn't going to be responsible for sending a woman to an army camp.

Because of her advertising scheme, the more Cleveland businesses she managed to name in her column, the more money she made. To scrape together the money required to get herself to the border as a free agent, she squeezed in as many advertising shout-outs as she could in the coming weeks. After all, she would need all kinds of things for her expedition: sturdy luggage, for example, and good boots for hiking. Not to mention the perfect restaurant for an extravagant send-off dinner with friends the night before her departure, and the beautiful dresses it would break her heart to leave behind.

When she went to an Ohio training camp to do her reporting in anticipation of the journey, she was the lone woman in a crowd of twelve thousand men. She claimed to have forgotten for brief moments that she would not be fighting alongside the soldiers there. Between training sessions, Peggy furiously wrote her articles; she felt she had discovered her life's purpose in war reporting.

As she left for the border, her farewell words to Cleveland readers sounded very much like a soldier's good-bye: "When I come back, I want to feel that you are all here waiting for me and that you have not forgotten me."

While on the border, Peggy persuaded a commander to let her go along with twenty thousand soldiers on a fifteen-day hike into New Mexico. "When I finally gained his consent," she later told the Marysville, Kansas, *Advocate-Democrat*, "I knew my military career depended on that hike." In other words, if she didn't make it to the end of the hike, or if she embarrassed herself in any way, she could forget ever persuading any commander to let her tag along on future expeditions. But, on the other hand, if she stuck it out, she might prove her hardiness and commitment once and for all.

She woke up at 4:00 a.m., put on her uniform—a wool skirt, a flannel shirt, and an army hat—and marched out the door to the sound of a bugle blowing. She was busy daydreaming about the journalistic acclaim that she would earn as a result of this hike when she tripped over a boulder, landing in a bush on the side of the road.

The next sign of trouble was a pain in her feet. It spread from her feet to her legs, and from her legs to her back. She lagged behind with a few straggling soldiers who struggled to keep up as well. The members of this unfortunate crew offered one another words of encouragement, helping each other make it to camp that night. When she finally made it, she was so tuckered out that she fell asleep on the floor of her tent before dinner.

Day two was not much easier. The hikers encountered a brutal sandstorm. "I felt as though I had never had a bath," Peggy wrote. She seriously questioned her desire for a career as a military correspondent at this point, but she had talked other people into letting her do this, and she knew that giving up was not an option.

On day four, she finally received her first sign of much-needed validation. "Private Hull," a voice said while she was in line for dinner. She turned around. "You have been promoted to the rank of first lieutenant."

When she got to her hotel in the border town where the troops were stationed, she was proud—and exhausted. She saw her silky soft nightgown in a heap on the bed and could not wait to curl up in it and drift comfortably off to sleep.

She did not go with the troops across the border into Mexico, but she waited eagerly to witness their return. Meanwhile she covered life on the border, but because the Ohio boys weren't around and she hadn't been in Cleveland in such a long time that keeping up her advertising column was no longer possible, she went and found a job with a local El Paso paper, letting go of her home base in Cleveland altogether. With that, Peggy became a Texan—but not for long.

When the United States declared war on Germany, Peggy was determined, once again, to march in lockstep with her country's armed forces. Steeling herself with an answer to every objection, she walked into her managing editor's office and asked to be sent to France as a war correspondent. Her editor was shocked at the preposterous suggestion. Not only was she a woman, but this was a small paper with a circulation of twenty-five thousand. Send her to France? Was she out of her mind?

Maybe. But she did not leave his office until she had talked him into it.

Peggy had a lot of things to do before going abroad to report from a war zone beyond getting authorization. She thought these steps would be easier than getting her editor's permission, but she was wrong. She went to New York, where her first order of business was getting a passport from the State Department, and her second order of business was getting the two visas she would need: one to work in England and another to work in France. For these, she would have to appeal to the British and French consulates.

Most of her male colleagues simply completed the paperwork and got their passports issued as a routine process that might involve some minor bureaucratic frustrations, but surely nothing more—assuming their credentials were in place. When Peggy submitted her paperwork, she was flat out denied. Her only recourse was to appear in person before a judge. Upon hearing this news, her male colleagues placed bets on whether she'd get her passport and head off to Europe, or if she'd have to travel back to Texas with her tail between her legs. The ordeal tested her nerve. She was physically trembling by the time she arrived to discuss her case, which made her question whether she really had the bravery this assignment would demand of her. "What a lot of useless emotion I was going through over a passport," she wrote to her readers back home in the *El Paso Morning Times.* "[If] I felt like this about the verdict how in the world would I feel if a submarine hit my ship?"

The meeting went smoothly. Peggy handed over copies of the *El Paso Morning Times* containing her work, and got her passport without having to put up a fight. Having earned the State Department's approval, she thought she'd sail through deliberations at the British and French consulate.

Wrong again. Peggy was not accredited as an official US war correspondent. The War Department had never granted a woman accreditation. Peggy's editor had reluctantly agreed to send her, and the State Department had reluctantly given its stamp of approval, but aside from that, she was on her own—no government protection, no one to usher her into army camps, no transportation provided. As a result, the British consul who reviewed her case was skeptical. He didn't understand why the paper she worked for would send a woman, especially one who had never been out of the country before. She listed her qualifications, detailing her border experiences with the Ohio National Guard. The consul sent her away empty-handed nonetheless. Refusing to accept this decision, Peggy requested that the State Department send the copies of the *El Paso Morning Times* that she had submitted for her passport. When she returned, the same consul who had given her a hard time on her first visit conceded, "Your paper is all right."

When she finally boarded her ocean liner, she was overcome with doubt. As a little girl, she'd imagined growing sweet peas in a garden, marrying a nice man, and raising children some day. As she embarked for the unknown, she wondered what on earth had prompted her to venture off to war, sleepless in an undulating ship cabin instead of drifting easily off to dreamland in a cozy bungalow back home. But she did her best to cling to her conviction that this was what she had been put on earth to do.

Peggy spent twelve days on the ocean liner, gradually adjusting to seasickness and to her British shipmates' funny way of talking. She was temporarily delayed in London, waiting for permission to continue on to France. While in London, she wrote cheeky articles about the idiosyncrasies of British life, including the way the British greet one another over the phone. Instead of "hello" they would say "who's thar?"—which utterly confused a jet-lagged Peggy. Back home, a reader from England who had settled in El Paso wrote to the paper, confessing that she had once believed this Peggy Hull character to be mythical, not real. Reading Peggy's accounts of life in Britain, however, she finally knew for sure that Peggy was not only real, but she was also really in England. Nobody could possibly capture London life so vividly from here in the States, she asserted. Reading Peggy's columns transported her back home.

When Peggy finally arrived in Paris, she checked into her hotel then went straight out to a sidewalk cafe in hopes of absorbing the atmosphere in war-torn Paris. She had barely arrived when she witnessed the American troops marching into the city. Making the scene that much more powerful, it happened to be the Fourth of July. Peggy reported that the arrival of American troops instantly changed the mood on the streets of Paris from dismal and gray to celebratory and hopeful.

Her inability to understand the French language put her in all kinds of humorous situations—as well as a few dangerous ones. She was reading in bed one night when the power suddenly went out, and she heard sirens. It was an air raid. She ran into the hallway of her hotel but could not understand what people were frantically saying to her. Finally, not knowing what to do, she ran back into her bedroom and hid under her blankets, covering her head with all she had: a pillow.

Eventually, Peggy's war coverage got the attention of papers outside of El Paso. She started contributing to the *Army Tribune*—read by soldiers—and to the *Chicago Tribune* and other US papers. She got busier and busier, but her lack of accreditation still resulted in missed opportunities. But in place of opportunities that were simply handed to other correspondents, Peggy went out looking for opportunities of her own—and found them. This is what made her stories unique.

She went on a road trip to small villages dangerously close to the front lines, and she even stayed in an army barracks and in an army hospital, where she heard the shrieks of a wounded soldier in surgery one night. When she walked through the camp in a white fur coat with an American flag pinned to it, American soldiers saluted her as though she were a general.

Once again giddy at her intimacy with the American soldier's experience, she wrote, "I've lived in a tent. I'm living in barracks. . . . There is nothing I don't know about being a soldier in France except how it feels to live like a general."

Admittedly, she also carried a sewing kit with her to the front so that she could assist the troops with repairing the buttons on their uniforms.

Before long, the inside connections Peggy developed and the special access her inside sources granted her caused other correspondents to stop seeing her as a novelty. They started seeing her not as an equal, but as a threat. They complained about her to the authorities and demanded that she be sent home.

Peggy was not sent home, but given the hostile climate, she decided to return home on her own. She wrote a scathing farewell letter, which was printed in the *El Paso Morning Times* on December 13, 1918. Concluding the letter, she assured her jealous colleagues that when the war was over, if they needed jobs, they could always join her in El Paso. And she promised to be gracious should their stories ever push hers off the front page.

Peggy made a true soldier's return home to El Paso. She was invited to speak before groups of businessmen about her experiences, and drew standing ovations from all her crowds. She wasn't done reporting from abroad. She also reported on World War II, by which point she had paved the way for other female war correspondents to go along with her.

Still it would be a long time before women taking dangerous jobs in journalism would be considered anything other than laughable. Peggy Hull did it before it was fashionable and long before there was anything even resembling a movement.

She even did it in uniform.

OSA JOHNSON

(1894–1953)

BOLD ADVENTURER, WORLD TRAVELER . . .
AND HOMEBODY AT HEART?

It is hard to imagine any definition of the word *homebody* that fits Osa Johnson.

Born in Chanute, Kansas, in 1894, Osa spent most of her adult life living in the African wilderness, collaborating with her husband—explorer Martin Johnson—on nine feature-length films, seventeen short films, and thousands of still photographs. The couple observed and documented animals, cultures, and natural settings the Western world had previously only imagined. Osa shot game, caught fish, filmed wild lions without benefit of a zoom lens, flew her own plane, and shot a charging elephant to save her husband's life.

Nonetheless, a homebody is exactly what she claimed to be. "In reality I am a homebody," she wrote in an article for *Collier's.* "'Home' has come to mean to me not a fixed spot somewhere in civilization, but an expedition into the wilds. . . . I make a home on the go."

A home on the go may not have been what her parents had in mind for her. Osa began her autobiography, *I Married Adventure,* by describing what she calls the "placid expectation" of girls born in late nineteenth century Chanute—that is, the expectation that they would grow up, marry, raise a family, and die without ever leaving town.

Such was not her fate. Dark-haired and doe-eyed, Osa Leighty was, in most ways, an ordinary Kansas girl growing up. A local farmer said of her that she was "very attractive in a dark, petite sort of way. But there was nothing about her to make you think she would ever care to become a crack shot and at home in the depths of Africa."

Osa met her future husband for the first time when she was only seven years old. Martin Johnson, back then, was a wandering teen photographer who had dropped out of school and was traveling from Kansas town to Kansas town photographing locals in small rented studios. Photography was still a new invention, and portraits were rare treasures. They were hard to come by, and they were expensive. Osa begged her parents for a dime to take her baby brother for a portrait. They reluctantly obliged. Osa dressed her little brother so he would look dignified for the photo, but before the portrait was taken, her brother started fussing. Johnson—remembering how *he* had hated wearing collars as a little boy—removed the boy's collar. The informality of the portrait for which she had paid a dime infuriated young Osa. She spent many years seething at the nerve of that bull-headed traveling photographer, whose name she never knew.

Years later, Johnson came back through town on tour with a slide show of photographs he had taken during his adventure as cook on Jack London's boat, the *Snark,* which had traveled to the South Seas. Johnson had been selected from a huge pool of applicants for this spot on London's expedition, and he hoped that this would be the beginning of a life of travel and adventure. And though he was hired to cook, his real interest had been capturing vivid images of exotic people and places to wow the folks back home. When Mr. London came down with dysentery and fever, the trip was cut short. Martin began touring the United States with his picture shows, daydreaming about picking up where the *Snark* had left off.

Osa attended Martin's screening, not because she was interested in this proud man's travels, but because her friend Gail sang at the theater before all the Saturday films. Osa's main purpose in going to the movies was to applaud her friend. She claimed to have spent her future husband's entire presentation fantasizing about ice cream.

Gail introduced Martin and Osa, but the introduction didn't take at first. In fact, it failed to "take" many times over. It was not until Gail asked

Osa Johnson Martin and Osa Johnson Safari Museum, Chanute, Kansas

Osa to fill in as preshow entertainment at one of Martin's theaters that Osa and Martin truly got to know one another, and they quickly bonded. Equally strong willed, they finally met their match in one another.

Osa's grandmother immediately expressed concern that Osa was taking up with a man who had traveled to so many faraway places. Who could say how many dirty little secrets might litter his strange and distant path? But familial disapproval didn't slow the determined couple down one bit. Martin and Osa simply eloped and spent their honeymoon on the road, sleeping in rooming houses, train stations, and even on a pool table in one mining town.

Osa had always imagined that once she married, life would roll along "smoothly with pleasant monotony to the grave." For a very brief time, in keeping with expectations, Osa and Martin tried settling down like an ordinary couple. They accumulated fine china. They grew restless and unhappy.

It wasn't long before they threw in the dainty dish towel and began traveling, this time as a couple. In every town they visited, they found a theater and performed a vaudeville act, collecting the cost of admission and then picking up and moving on, doing it all over again in a different town the very next day. They weren't trying to become stars of the stage, though Osa was supposedly not bad at the Hawaiian dances she performed. Their goal was to raise money to fund an overseas adventure. This time, they would go together, as a husband-and-wife team. They would not apply for spots on someone else's expedition. They would do it on their own.

When their families discovered that rather than sticking around Kansas, the couple planned to go off in search of the most dangerous people and animals in the world, they were beside themselves. Their wrath was directed at Martin, who, in their estimation, failed to understand his duty as husband. Osa recalled that Martin's father said to him, "It's alright, son, for you to go and risk your neck, but I don't think you've any right to risk hers."

The notion that Osa would not *want* to go on this adventure, that she was an unwilling participant, offended her deeply. She had worked hard and spent miserable holidays away from her beloved family back home in order to raise money for the trip. The only thing that kept her going during these hardscrabble times was her desire to be a part of an exciting adventure overseas, an adventure that she and her husband would share. The idea of not going after all the sacrifices she had made frustrated and upset her.

Every time Martin expressed doubts about what he had dragged her into, she protested furiously. When the couple faced financial ruin during their vaudeville tour, the ever-resourceful Osa took to running a boardinghouse on the side. Martin was embarrassed that his wife was supporting him and not the other way around. The day she took in her first roomers, he got serious about booking theaters for their show. When he succeeded, he came home and told her to forget about their flop-house for the night. They were going to stay at the Waldorf to celebrate.

"Oh no, we're not," she remembers telling him. "If you have half the brains I give you credit for, I think you'll save that money and buy a motion picture camera and go around the world."

By the time they were ready to leave home, she saw the trip to the South Seas as a shared adventure she had chosen and earned, though it was a far cry from any future she had envisioned for herself. The goal was to bring home film footage of wild animals and faraway people. Osa was not merely a companion; she was a partner. The responsibilities she assumed would prove crucial to the completion of the work they set out to do and to their survival in the wilderness.

Of course, the integral nature of her role on the expedition did nothing to allay her parents' fears. Her father believed she would face financial ruin, losing her shirt and her dreams in one crushing blow. Her mother believed she would die on this treacherous journey, succumbing to fever, or—worse—being devoured by cannibals, who would boil her or possibly eat her alive, not even taking the trouble to cook her. What on earth did a good Kansas girl want with cannibals, anyway? Her parents could not understand what motivated their daughter.

In a 1919 telegram to her worried parents as she left for the South Seas and Africa, Osa the Homebody wrote, "Dear Mother and Father, We are off today for the south seas with the determination to bring back the most wonderful pictures ever made." She added, ". . . Now darlings be good and remember the years will soon roll bye [*sic*] and then I won't take any more trips."

After some initial disappointment at the tameness of the first leg of their trip to the South Seas, Osa and Martin learned of an island called Malekula where cannibalism reportedly prevailed. Martin—who was now under pressure to stage the kind of scene he had set out to find— was beside himself with excitement. He was determined to go, but he told Osa that he couldn't risk taking her along to such a dangerous place.

Osa was enraged. Her heart pounded something awful.

"If you go," she insisted, "I'm going with you. . . . That's what I came for and that's how it's going to be the whole way. The whole way!" Martin heard her and understood that there would be no arguing with Osa on this point. She did go with him the whole way, not just on this trip, but for the duration of their lives together.

Although the Johnsons expected all kinds of savagery upon arriving in Malekula, they were politely received by a man with a distended belly and a stomachache. They won him over by offering him pain relief tablets. Martin filmed the islanders as they showed the couple around. Everything seemed to be going swimmingly until they reached the island's interior, where the tribe's chief resided.

The tone changed dramatically when the couple was suddenly surrounded by men with guns. Martin kept filming, even as he and Osa believed they had been taken captive and that their lives were in extreme danger. If the couple did not survive, Martin reasoned, the film footage might. He caught headhunters on film, treating and preserving human heads on skewers. When they managed to get away from the island, badly dehydrated and in desperate need of nourishment, they were upset. Not by their close brush with mortality, however. No, they were distraught only that their film had been exposed to heat and humidity far exceeding normal conditions; bringing home documentation had been the point all along. The possibility that the film had been damaged made them both sick with disappointment. Some of the film footage from Malekula did survive and can still be viewed today, but much of it was ruined.

Upon returning from this trying adventure on which Martin and Osa had only each other and their belief in the importance of their work together, Martin received a letter from the resident commissioner from New Hebrides. In the letter, the commissioner stated that he had heard of Martin's plans to penetrate the interior of the island of Malekula, and he warned Martin that he could not make such a trip without considerable risk to himself and those accompanying him. The letter urged him not to proceed, and concluded with the line, "In any case I trust you will not take your wife into the danger zone with you."

The commissioner trusted wrong.

Upon returning to the United States with their footage, the Johnsons became minor celebrities and caught the attention of an anthropologist at the American Museum of Natural History in New York. He had long hoped to create an African wing for his museum, and his first step would be procuring documentation of wild herds of African animals as they currently existed, before they faced what he assumed would be eventual extinction in the face of European settlement and safaris—opportunities for the white man to prove himself on the African terrain, regardless of the effect of his hobbies on that very continent.

The museum funded the Johnsons' next expedition, this time to Africa with the goal of capturing native animals on film in their natural habitat. Having never focused specifically on wildlife photography before, the couple learned the hard way that a wild animal has one of only two reactions to a camera: run away from it or run toward it. Neither yields great photographs. The couple devised solutions to this problem that revolutionized nature photography, and gave birth to the wildlife documentary genre. Most significantly, they learned that they could not go to the animals; they needed the animals to come to them. In order to bring this scenario about, they painstakingly and laboriously built hideouts near watering holes. Animals would come to the water to drink, and Martin and Osa would be waiting for them, hidden from view for as long as possible. The footage they captured is still shocking: Crocodiles thrash in the water so close to the camera that water splashes on the lens, and the animal's movement is so immediate that it practically feels as though the animal is slithering beneath the living room couch. Herds of zebras gallop across the savannah, raising dirt beneath them. Elephants stride in a slow, indifferent shuffle, wrinkly skin drooping over their stealthy frames, plants and sticks crackling beneath the weight of their giant feet. Gazelles leap so fast they're gone almost as soon as they appear. Rhinos let out low deep moans that shake viewers to their bones. Lions' tails swish with the tall grass in the breeze.

When the couple found a map in an old book indicating that there was a hidden lake in a mountain crater, off they went in search of it. If it existed, it would be the only water for fifty miles surrounded by desert, making it an animal-stalking mecca. When they found it, Osa called it Lake Paradise. They moved in, set up camp, and stayed for four years, bringing in a team and building amenities such as filtered water, electricity, and a photo lab that rivaled anything found back in the states. Animals came in the hundreds, giving it what Osa called a "Noah's Ark unreality."

Osa created a flower and vegetable garden, only instead of finding it visited in the night by pesky rabbits and squirrels, she witnessed an elephant eating her sweet potatoes. Gorillas ate her celery. She also hunted game and fished, providing for herself and Martin in a primitive, hunter-gatherer way. Martin spent his day filming wildlife. Osa shot it in her own way.

In an article titled "I Was Almost Cannibal Stew," published in *Popular Science* in 1929, Martin wrote about a day during this stint when the couple filmed lions in Africa, aiming to bring home an accurate and empathetic representation of how the supposedly ferocious lion really lived and behaved. The result is a film called *Simba: King of the Beasts.*

"Usually I worked unarmed," Martin wrote of the outings to gather this footage, "cranking away at the camera while Mrs. Johnson gaged [*sic*] how close she dare let death approach. Many a time I have thanked God that Osa held the gun."

On this particular day, Osa let death come awfully close, waiting not just until her husband was actually being charged by a wild lion, but in fact, allowing Martin to capture the lion charging toward him on film before defending him. Then, and only then, did she come to his aid.

"A lion charges at a speed unequaled by another wild animal," Martin asserted. "It has been estimated that he covers the last hundred yards of his charge in about 3 seconds! I can't say I enjoyed standing there turning my crank during that rush. It was the most beautiful, yet terrifying sight I think I have ever seen. The lion looked as big as a full-grown bull as he came tearing down upon us, his mane flying and his dripping teeth bared for the final death-dealing assault. Osa did not flinch."

More famously, Osa once protected her husband from a charging elephant. Martin calls this moment "one of the closest shaves I ever had."

He wrote, "She saw the peril I was in. But we had long since schooled ourselves to get the film first and save our lives afterward. . . . She kept turning the crank. She knew she was getting the greatest wild elephant picture ever taken."

When it came time to defend herself and her husband, Osa's task was of both critical importance and utmost difficulty. Martin explains: "Her target was physically as big as a barn. But she had to hit a spot the size of my hand, and hit it in the half-second during which it was moving at high speed across her line of vision. Once more, her cool sharp eye saved my life."

According to the curators at the Safari Museum in Chanute, Kansas, Osa fired one warning shot, and when the elephant forged on undeterred, she shot the tusked giant on her first try. He collapsed on the camera tripod—that is how close she had allowed him to get. Osa saw the elephant's foot as a personal trophy of sorts; it now sits on display in the Safari Museum for visitors to see.

Osa's rule of thumb was never to shoot unless it was an absolute necessity. "We promised each other to stick to the camera until it became certain that we must either desert it or perish," she wrote in an article titled "My Home in the African Blue" later, "and never to shoot until we were sure that it was an animal's life or one of ours."

But when she did shoot an animal, she used all of it. She had the skin of a zebra sent back home to be transformed into shoes and a belt, which she wore proudly on returning to New York. She was named one of the best-dressed women of her time, but she earned as many detractors as fans for her fashion sensibility. She was seen by some as that woman who ran around in the African wilderness looking for animal pelts to wear.

Although Osa liked to dress well, such pleasures were nothing to her compared to exploring unknown lands. The American city, despite its many comforts, had lost its appeal by comparison. It is in this sense that she was, as she claimed, a homebody.

"I am restless and vaguely unhappy in New York," she wrote. "It is a city that fills me with wants."

Remarkably, Osa never saw her own bravery as remarkable. In fact she barely even acknowledged that her bravery was brave.

"I am not a very brave person," she wrote. "I know I do a great many things that seem courageous to women who have never been put to the test. . . . It is the unexpected that puts your bravery to the test."

As for her gritty starlet status, she preferred it to any of the other kinds of starlet status a woman of her time could hope to achieve. She took pride in being hard and mean, not soft and sweet. Her most often quoted statement that survived even after Osa herself was largely forgotten is the following:

"A woman that's too soft and sweet is like tapioca pudding—fine for them as likes it."

AMELIA EARHART

(1897–?)

CELEBRITY, GREAT UNSOLVED MYSTERY, AND POSSIBLE CASTAWAY

"Some elders have to be shocked for everybody's good now and then."
—AMELIA EARHART

Pilot Amelia Earhart is one of the best-remembered women in this book—and, in fact, in all of American history. Ironically one of her major claims to fame is that nobody knows how her story ended; her plane, the *Electra,* lost contact with ground control and disappeared somewhere over the Pacific Ocean. Exactly where, exactly why, and whether she survived the crash remain mysteries.

But every good story starts at the beginning, so let's back up and answer a simpler question—where did Amelia Earhart come from?—before getting to the prickly, multimillion-dollar question of where she ended up.

Amelia Earhart was born in Atchison, Kansas, at the end of the nineteenth century. Although she went to school in Atchison up until her high school years, Amelia's father was a railroad man, and at the time, railroads threaded through the country, branching off and reaching even the unlikeliest places. As a result, his work took him to the nation's furthest extremities. When a trip took him away for any significant amount of time, he did not leave his family behind. Instead, he packed up his wife, Amelia, and Amelia's sister, Muriel, and took them with him to California, Kansas City, Des Moines, Chicago, St. Paul, and other places, where they would all live until the job ended. Amelia grew up knowing that the world was a big place, that there were fascinating people to meet

Amelia Earhart Kansas Historical Society

out there, and that none of it was out of her reach. And she claimed that these interruptions from school never interfered with her education. In fact, she believed she gained as much from travel as she would have from school curriculum.

But when asked what it was about her childhood that set the stage for her career as a daredevil pilot, eager to make a daredevil trip around the world, the other thing Amelia was quick to mention was always "liking all kinds of sports and games" and "not being afraid to try those that some of my elders in those days looked upon as being only for boys."

Amelia and Muriel were the first two girls in Atchison to have what were known as gymnasium suits, or simply gym suits. In the late 1800s, physicians and private women's colleges in the Northeast began vocally encouraging more rigorous exercise for women and girls. Previously, they had only been encouraged to do mild calisthenics, and for the small gentle movements required of them, they wore skirts and dresses. The suggestion that women take on more demanding kinds of exercise for health and recreation pushed the women to get up and get moving. It also inspired a demand for more appropriate women's athletic attire— appropriate not in the sense of being "ladylike" but in the sense of being suitable for running and jumping and roughhousing and mayhem. For a while, a costume made out of flannel that consisted of an ankle-length skirt hiding trousers, or bloomers, was popular. Letting the bottoms of one's pant legs peek out below the hem of one's skirt was considered quite randy. But when basketball came into the picture, this outfit simply wouldn't do the trick. It was too bulky.

Basketball was invented in 1891. Believe it or not, basketball—like the light bulb and the printing press and the cotton gin—had to be invented. It was different from the sports that already existed because it was a game of skill and not just strength.

The sport spread like wildfire through the athletics departments of schools nationwide, and women and girls took it up enthusiastically.

They shot hoops with reckless abandon. And they needed outfits that would allow them to move quickly. Their old-fashioned getups forced them to carry around a bunch of extra fabric that slowed them down and tripped them up.

Enter the gym suit: long wide shorts that mimicked a skirt on the bottom and a wide, airy blouse on top. In the middle, at the waist, a belt held the whole number together.

When Amelia and her sister Muriel went out in their gym suits, they were way ahead of the sports and fashion trends in Atchison, Kansas. "We wore them on Saturdays," Amelia recalled in her 1932 memoir *The Fun of It: Random Records of My Own Flying and of Women in Aviation*, "and though we felt terribly free and athletic, we also felt somewhat as outcasts among the little girls who fluttered about us in their skirts."

Amelia liked basketball, tennis, and bicycling, all of which were still frowned upon as pastimes for girls. And because competitive sports were not yet considered mainstream activities for girls, they were not taught to girls. So young Amelia taught herself to play. Sure, her technique was a little wanting, but she wasn't the type to wait for an invitation to do something she thought might be fun. And she didn't let an unladylike costume or a missed chance to take lessons interfere with the pleasure she derived from sports.

Amelia didn't walk home from school like the other kids: She *ran*. And she didn't use the gate to the fence surrounding her house. That just didn't seem efficient. Instead, she jumped the fence as though it were a hurdle. Her obstacle-course approach to getting home from school got her inside the front door in record time, every time. She was very proud of her speed.

Her grandmother worried terribly about the behavior. Little girls weren't supposed to jump fences. "You don't realize," Amelia recalls her saying, "that when I was a small girl, I did nothing more strenuous than roll my hoop in the public square."

For a while, Amelia took the long way home—through the gate, and not over the fence. But not for long. She just couldn't stand to walk when she knew she could run.

The barn outside the house was crawling with critters, which did not scare Amelia or her sister. Amelia and Muriel asked for popguns for Christmas. Using the popguns, the girls shot rats out in the barn for sheer entertainment. That must have shocked Grandma as well.

By the time she finished high school, Amelia had relocated to Chicago with the rest of the Earhart clan, and graduated from Hyde Park High—the sixth high school she attended while zigzagging the country with the railroads.

Amelia was no prom queen. Of her teenage romantic endeavors, all she said was this: "I don't think that boys particularly cared for me, but I can't remember being very sad about the situation."

The boys' lack of interest in her would change by the time she embarked upon adulthood. In fact, some say that her attractiveness was in part responsible for her notoriety as a pilot. The slender woman with short, tousled, honey-colored hair, piercing eyes, and easy grin had a confident whimsy about her that went straight to the heart of the American public. But it certainly wasn't what Amelia wanted to be known for, and it certainly had nothing to do with her decision to learn how to fly.

Between graduating from high school and earning her pilot's license, Amelia did a lot of things. She attended college briefly, but, preferring action to reflection, she gave that up to work as a nurse's aid in a Toronto hospital during World War I. Her main selling point, as a nurse's aide, was the fact that she knew a little chemistry and could be trusted not to help herself to the medicinal whiskey.

It was around this time that she became interested in airplanes. Before World War I, the only planes she saw were at county fairs. Civilians did not fly. But America's involvement in World War I meant that pilots and officers required training, and Amelia—like all Americans—began seeing planes with more regularity. In the winter of 1918, Amelia stood outside, snow collecting on her face, and was mesmerized as she watched the training sessions with a sense of longing. The training she got on the sidelines was far from perfect, but the inspiration was solid. A lifelong love affair with airplanes had officially begun, and Amelia would soon be swept off her feet.

When the war was over and the need for nurse's aides diminished, Amelia resumed her college career, imagining that she would study medicine. But as she learned the trade, she had a vision of herself at the bedside of a hypochondriac offering placebos instead of real medicine. The practices she was learning rang false, and she began to feel that practicing medicine would make a phony of her. Again she left college, and she joined her parents in California, unsure what she would do next.

Her intention was to finish college in California, but before she got around to it, she got involved with airplanes again. At first she just stalked her beloved planes, visiting airfields and watching others fly them. She dragged her father to an air circus and sent him to ask the pilot questions about flying—like how long did it take to learn to fly, and how much did the lessons cost—but she was too self-conscious to approach a pilot herself. Then one fateful day at an airfield in a suburb of Los Angeles, she got up her nerve and talked the pilot into letting her on board as a passenger for a short flight. That was all it took to win her over completely.

She remembers going home that night and announcing to her family that she wanted to fly. When the response was casual and supportive, the stunned Amelia set about signing up for lessons, then came back to her parents asking for help to pay for them. Her parents were equally stunned; they hadn't realized their daughter was serious.

Her parents' unwillingness to front her the cash didn't stop Amelia, just as feeling unladylike in a gym suit hadn't stopped her and her grandmother's admonitions against fence jumping only slowed her down for a few days before she was right back at it. Amelia got a job at a telephone company and paid for the flying lessons herself. She worked all week long and then spent her entire weekend in a dusty airfield outside of town.

"My learning to fly was a rather long-drawn-out process," she wrote, "principally because—no pay, no fly and no work, no pay."

Taking the scenic route probably worked to her advantage. She invested years of hard work and commitment, so that by the time she finally got to fly, she felt so overdue for the experience that all nervousness had vanished. She experienced pure excitement and nothing else. Other than an exceptionally bad landing, the flight went smoothly. Once she had been up in the air and came home in one piece, proving both her determination and her ability, her mother caved in and helped her pay for a secondhand plane of her own.

A year later, Amelia received her pilot's license from the Fédération Aéronautique Internationale.

At the time when Amelia learned to fly, air travel was totally unfamiliar to the ordinary American. A number of people told her they would like to fly close to the ground first—which those who have flown know is actually a more terrifying prospect than being up in the clouds. Takeoff and landing are the scariest, most dramatic parts of flying, even for passengers, for that very reason. Some people weren't just afraid of flying; they were afraid to even look at airplanes. A friend of Amelia's once confessed to her that she closed her eyes every time she saw a plane because she was afraid that looking at it would make her dizzy.

In an eerily prophetic statement, Amelia pointed out, "Trouble in the air is very rare. . . . Sometimes a cautious pilot elects to come down at once to make a minor engine adjustment. Something is wrong and very properly he is unwilling to risk flying further, even though he may be able to do so. . . . All of which obviously points to the necessity of providing frequent landing places along all the airways. Few things, I think, would do more to eliminate accidents in the air."

Amelia Earhart took up aviation as a personal passion, not a profession. It wasn't her day job. She did other things for a living. For example, she worked as a social worker for a while, and it was at the home where she worked that she got a phone call in the middle of the day from one Captain H. H. Riley, who told her about an opportunity to be the first American woman to fly across the Atlantic—as a passenger. Another woman had planned and funded the trip, but at the last minute, she was unable to go on her own publicity stunt. Captain Riley encouraged Amelia to go to New York to find out if she was eligible.

What made a woman eligible to fly as a mere passenger on this highly publicized flight? Amelia remarked with a hearty dose of sarcasm that she never knew for sure, though others have suggested that her bubbly personality, her good looks, and a name that was too good to be true (*Earhart* is pronounced "air-heart") probably didn't hurt. Neither did her pilot's license, though of course she did not get to put it to much use. She was not the pilot. She was precious cargo.

"It was made clear that the men in the flight were being paid. Having established that, I was asked if I was prepared to receive no remuneration myself," she later recalled. "I said 'yes.' . . . My own compensation was . . . opportunities in aviation, writing and the like which the Atlantic crossing opened up for me."

A woman in flight was big news. It was such a public relations coup that Amelia's participation had to be hush-hush until a formal announcement was made. As such, she couldn't spend a lot of time looking over the aircraft, called *Friendship,* before takeoff. It would have aroused suspicion.

She expressed to the selection committee that she wished to do some flying herself, but any hope she had of actually doing so was dashed by unexpected weather conditions that only experts—meaning people who had seen the plane's controls more than once—could maneuver. She later claimed to have felt like a "sack of potatoes."

The rest of the world did not see her role that way. To people following the story, she embodied courage and daring. George Putnam, the promoter of the transatlantic flight who had published writings by Charles Lindbergh just a few years earlier, saw a great publishing opportunity in Earhart's adventure. He published the book she wrote upon her return: *20 Hours, 40 Minutes*.

The two were married in 1931, with Amelia continuing a career in aviation and George serving as her promoter and event planner. In truth, Amelia was as much a professional celebrity as she was a professional pilot. Civilian air travel was about to take off, and Amelia Earhart was on the forefront of that development. As ordinary people began to consider flying, she was one step ahead of them, telling them what it was like in her extremely popular magazine stories.

Amelia Earhart was a good pilot and a fast pilot—not the best pilot, not a full-time pilot. A good pilot. She had made impressive time, in some cases breaking records for speed, for her flights across North America, and she had been the first person to fly solo from California to Hawaii, from Los Angeles to Mexico City, and from Mexico City to Newark. Still, a trip around the world was an ambitious stunt. And a dangerous one.

Since 1989 Ric Gillespie has been looking for Earhart's remains through the organization TIGHAR (The International Group for Historic Aircraft Recovery) and is the author of *Finding Amelia: The True Story of the Earhart Disappearance*. He says of Earhart and her crew, "They were toast when they left the ground."

Amelia had underestimated the difficulty of the Pacific leg of the trip, he explains, and the people who might have been in a position to tell her so—the officers of the Coast Guard, for example—actively avoided involvement in setting up this trip. Amelia had a reputation for not doing as she was told, and nobody wanted to be blamed if something went wrong. Kinks in communication between her plane, the *Electra*, and the

US Coast Guard cutter *Itasca* on the ground were not sufficiently ironed out before takeoff. Amelia indicated she would use Greenwich time, for example, and the crew on the *Itasca* did not get the message and therefore interpreted many of her requests incorrectly. Likewise, Amelia did not know the limitations of *Itasca*'s ability to take bearings on her plane using radio signals. Foreseeable problems and communication details went unaddressed prior to and after takeoff. It was just too late.

Amelia's reputation—deserved or not, sexist or not—put her in peril in more ways than one. While up in the air, in the day or so before her plane disappeared on July 2, 1937, there were many instances where she did not respond to the people on the ground, and she did not do what they expected her to do. Rather than growing concerned that something had gone wrong or that communication was failing—which, it is now clear, was most certainly the case—they just grew frustrated, assuming she was either ignoring them, didn't know what she was doing, or some maddening combination of the two.

The crew aboard the *Itasca* could hear Amelia's radio transmissions, but she couldn't hear theirs. Confusion prevailed. Phrases like "We're drifting" baffled the crew. Drifting how? No answer. Requests to contact her in a half hour when a previous transmission claimed she would be out of fuel by then confounded people on the ground. Researchers now think that she said "on the half hour," not "in a half hour."

Despite countless communication malfunctions, one thing finally became abundantly clear: Amelia was lost.

On the morning that she was supposed to land at an airport on Howland Island in the central Pacific, a member of the crew wrote in a daily log, "The sky was partly cloudy, mostly with high scattered cumulus drifting slowly past. The *Itasca* kept in close to the lee of the island, sending out huge clouds of smoke to aid Miss Earhart in finding the island. Rescue parties were stationed on the runways and out in boats, while the official greeters waited anxiously at the reception spot. All eyes gazed fondly, proudly, and eagerly over the horizons." Everyone expected to see her plane any moment. Faces pointed skyward in anticipation.

The last message the *Itasca* received from Amelia before arriving at the conclusion that her plane had surely gone down could read like a routine transmission if you consider strictly *what* she said. She said, "KHAQQ to *Itasca*. We are on the line 157 337. We will repeat message. We will repeat this on 6210 kilocycles. Wait." Pause. "We are running on line north and south."

There was nothing terribly remarkable in what she said. What was remarkable was how she said it. One official report described her communication as "hurried, frantic, and apparently not complete."

One of the men on the *Itasca* remembered hearing her voice on that final transmission years later. "She sounded as if she would have broken out into a scream," he recalled. "She was just about ready to break into tears and go into hysterics. That's exactly the way I'd describe her voice, now. I'll never forget it."

When Ric Gillespie started TIGHAR in 1985, he did so without the slightest interest in looking for Amelia Earhart's plane, the *Electra*. In fact he did everything he could to avoid it. Too much baggage, he thought, and too much hype. But you know what happens to the one person who isn't looking for something: On a fishing boat, it's the one person who doesn't like fish who's bound to catch the first bite. And among historic aircraft enthusiasts, Ric Gillespie was the fisherman who didn't care for fish. He wanted nothing to do with solving the Amelia Earhart mystery, which makes him, in a roundabout way, the most logical person to stumble upon new clues.

People at social gatherings and public appearances would ask him about Amelia Earhart, and he would tell them, "Look, she was almost certainly lost, and the technology doesn't exist to find such a small plane in such a large ocean. It's a media circus, we want nothing to do with it." When some trusted colleagues informed him that there was compelling evidence suggesting Amelia had landed on a specific uninhabited island and that nobody had looked for her there, he couldn't believe it was true. "Are you guys telling me that nobody has looked for Amelia Earhart in the most obvious place?" he asked.

Indeed, they were. Technological advances had been able to indicate more or less where Earhart *should* have been when she went down. At about that same location was an island. On this island, the navy had observed signs of recent habitation, even though the island had supposedly remained unpopulated since 1892. For some strange reason, nobody had gone to this island to thoroughly investigate whether there might be a correlation. That realization inspired Ric Gillespie to take on the case he had adamantly avoided for his entire career.

In three expeditions—the first in 2001, the second in 2007, and the third in 2010—TIGHAR found a lot of hints that suggested to Ric Gillespie that Amelia had been there for quite some time: a campsite replete with remains of a fire pit and the animals cooked and eaten there, along with glass cosmetic bottles made in the United States in the 1930s. Even though there are no other known castaways who would have been traveling with American women's cosmetics at that time, that doesn't amount to surefire proof—proof beyond a shadow of a doubt—that this campsite was the final dwelling of Amelia Earhart. It looks like that was probably the case, but that probably isn't good enough. Gillespie is still looking for indisputable evidence. He is hoping to find DNA on a future expedition.

"It's like this castaway fell out of the sky," he muses, thinking about the mysterious person who set up camp on this uninhabited island. Then he pauses. "Well, maybe she *did*."

"What fascinates me," says Gillespie, "is that there seems to have been this whole chapter of her life that happened after everyone thought her life had ended. Here's this person who had lived in the public spotlight and suddenly she's as alone as a person can possibly be on a waterless island. How did she live? What was that like?"

If Ric Gillespie brings to a close the mystery surrounding where Amelia Earhart ended up, those will certainly be the next unanswered questions to explore.

For now, the final chapter of Amelia Earhart's story—assuredly the most interesting chapter—sits somewhere in the Pacific Ocean just waiting to be written.

BIBLIOGRAPHY

Lucy Hobbs Taylor

Enss, Chris. *The Doctor Wore Petticoats: Women Physicians of the Old West*. Guilford, CT: Globe Pequot Press, 2006.

Lucy Hobbs Taylor file. Watkins Community Museum of History of the Douglas County Historical Society, Lawrence, KS.

Stern, Madeleine B. *We the Women: Career Firsts of Nineteenth Century America*. Lincoln: University of Nebraska Press, 1994.

Wynbrant, James. *The Excruciating History of Dentistry: Toothsome Tales and Oral Oddities from Babylon to Braces*. London: Macmillan, 2000.

Carry Nation

Harvey, Bonnie C. *Carry A. Nation, Saloon-Smasher and Prohibitionist*. Berkeley Heights, NJ: Enslow, 2002.

Kansas Historical Society. "Kansas Memory." Accessed July 12, 2011. http://kansasmemory.org.

Kansas Historical Society Museum, Main Gallery Exhibit, Topeka, Kansas, 2010.

Taylor, Robert Lewis. *Vessel of Wrath: The Life and Times of Carry Nation*. New York, Dutton Adult (Penguin), 1966.

Mary Elizabeth Lease

Blumberg, Dorothy Rose. "Mary Elizabeth Lease, Populist Orator: A Profile." *Kansas History, Volume 1*. Topeka: Kansas State Historical Society, 1978.

Bright, Leta. "'Wichita Cyclone' Scrambled State Politics; Mary Elizabeth Lease Center of Populist Storm that Rocked Kansas During 1890s." *Wichita Eagle & Beacon Magazine*, July 16, 1961).

Carlson, Anna Matilda. *The Heritage of the Bluestem: A Romance of the Prairie*. Kansas City, MO: Burton, 1930.

Duncan, Kunigunde. "Wichita 'Joan of Arc' Was Power in State Politics: Mary Ellen Lease's Oratory Decisive in Election; Ideas Later Adopted into US Law." *Wichita Eagle Magazine,* December 18, 1955.

Edson, Charles L. "Advice to Raise 'Less Corn and More Hell' Still Good, Says Mary Ellen Lease at 78." *Kansas City Star,* March 29, 1931.

Hicks, John D. *The Populist Revolt.* Minneapolis: University of Minnesota Press, 1931.

Kansas Department of Transportation. "The History of Kansas Railroads." Accessed July 12, 2011. http://www.ksdot.org/burrail/rail/railroads/history.asp.

Knudson, Jerry. "Kansas Woman Led Voter Reform Movement." *Topeka Capital-Journal,* February 21, 1960.

Mary Lease file. Newspaper clippings collection. Kansas State Historical Society, Topeka, KS.

Nye, Russel Blaine. *Midwestern Progressive Politics: A Historical Study of Its Origins and Development, 1870–1958.* New York: Harper and Row, 1965.

Lilla Day Monroe

Kleiman, Dena. "How Pioneer Women Lived." *New York Times,* October 17, 1975.

Monroe, Lilla Day. "Some Woman Suffrage History: Address of Mrs. Lilla Day Monroe of Topeka at Pike's Pawnee Village, September 26, 1906." *Transactions of the Kansas State Historical Society,* vol. 10. Topeka: Kansas State Historical Society, 1908.

Stratton, Joanna L. *Pioneer Women: Voices from the Kansas Frontier.* New York: Simon and Schuster, 1982.

Susanna Madora Salter

Billington, Monroe. "Susanna Madora Salter, First Woman Mayor." *Kansas History Quarterly* 21, no. 3 (1954), 173–183. Topeka: Kansas State Historical Society.

Jost, Lora. *Kansas Murals: A Traveler's Guide.* Lawrence: University
   Press of Kansas, 2006.
Kansas City Journal, April 6, 1887.
Kansas City Times, April 4–7, 1887.
New York Times. "Susanna Salter Dead; First Woman Mayor in US was
   101." March 18, 1961.
Wishart, David J, ed. *Encyclopedia of the Great Plains.* Lincoln:
   University of Nebraska Press, 2004.

Ann Clarke
Abbot, Mrs. J. B. *Reminiscences of Mrs. J. B. Abbot.* Manuscript Collection.
   Slavery in Kansas file. Kansas Historical Society, Topeka. 1895.
Armstrong, John. *Reminiscences of Slave Days in Kansas.* Manuscript
   Collection. Slavery in Kansas file. Kansas Historical Society,
   Topeka. Circa 1895.
Hendrick, George, and Willene Hendrick, eds. *Fleeing for Freedom:
   Stories of the Underground Railroad as Told by Levi Coffin and
   William Still.* Chicago: Ivan R. Dee, 2004.
Lecompton Historical Society and Constitution Hall State Historic
   Site, "Historic Lecompton." www.lecomptonkansas.com.
Owen, Olive. *The Underground Railroad.* Manuscript Collection.
   Slavery in Kansas file. Kansas Historical Society, Topeka.

Harvey Girls
Anson, Lyman, and Clifford Funkhouser. "Cupid Rides the Rails,"
   American Mercury, September 1940.
Florence Harvey House Museum. 221 Marion Street, Florence, KS,
   66851. January 6, 2011.
Foster, George H. *The Harvey House Cook Book.* Lanham, MD: Taylor
   Trade Publishing, 1992.
The Harvey Girls. Directed by George Sidney. 1945. Burbank, CA:
   Warner Home Video, 2002. DVD, 102 minutes.

Henderson, James D. *Meals by Fred Harvey: A Phenomenon of the American West.* Fort Worth: Texas Christian University Press, 1969.

Morris, Judy. *Harvey Girls: The Women Who Civilized the West.* New York: Walker Books for Young Readers, 1996.

Paules, Greta Foff. *Dishing It Out: Power and Resistance Among Waitresses in a New Jersey Restaurant.* Philadelphia, PA: Temple University Press, 1992.

Poling-Kempis, Lesley. *The Harvey Girls: Women Who Opened the West.* New York: Marlowe, 1989.

Topeka Capital. "Harvey Tamed the West With Good Food, Pretty Girls." December 9, 1951.

Nora Holt

African-American Registry. "Nora Douglas Holt, a Musical Pioneer!" Accessed July 12, 2011. http://aaregistry.org.

Brown, Elsa Barkley, Darlene Clark Hine, and Rosalyn Terborg Penn. *Black Women in America: An Historical Encyclopedia.* Bloomington: Indiana University Press, 1994.

Holt, Nora, and Helen Walker-Hill, eds. *Five Interludes for Solo Piano.* St. Louis, MO: Vivace Press.

Kansas City, Kansas, Public Library. "Quindaro Exhibit." Accessed July 12, 2011. www.kckpl.lib.ks.us/kansas-collection/topic/quindaro-exhibit.aspx

Reed, Bill. *Hot from Harlem: Twelve African-American Entertainers, 1890–1960.* Jefferson, NC: McFarland Publishing, 2009.

Smith, Thaddeus T. "Western University: A Ghost College in Kansas." Master's thesis, Kansas State College, Pittsburg, KS, 1966.

Walker-Hill, Helen. *From Spirituals to Symphonies: African-American Women Composers and Their Music.* Westport, CT: Greenwood Press, 2002.

Ella Deloria

Boyer, Paul. *Native American Colleges, Progress and Prospects: An Ernest L. Boyer Project of the Carnegie Foundation for the Advancement of Teaching.* San Francisco: Jossey-Bass, 1997.

Deloria, Ella. Letter to Franz Boas, 1926. Ella Deloria Biographical File. Haskell Indian Nations University Museum and Cultural Center Archives, Lawrence, KS.

Deloria, Ella, and Raymond J. DeMillie. *Waterlily.* Lincoln: University of Nebraska Press, 1988.

Deloria, Ella, and Vine Deloria Jr. *Speaking of Indians.* Lincoln: University of Nebraska Press, 1998.

Erodes, Richard, and Alfonzo Ortiz, eds. *American Indian Myths and Legends.* New York: Pantheon, 1985.

Stille, Darlene R. *Extraordinary Women Scientists.* Chicago: Children's Press, 1995.

Vuckovic, Myriam. *Voices from Haskell: Indian Students between Two Worlds, 1884–1928.* Lawrence: University Press of Kansas, 2008.

Peggy Hull

Beasley, Maurine H., and Sheila J. Gibbons. *Taking Their Place: A Documentary History of Women and Journalism.* Washington DC: American University Press in cooperation with the Women's Institute for Freedom of the Press, 1993.

Bogart, Eleanor A., and Wilda M. Smith. *The Wars of Peggy Hull: The Life and Times of a War Correspondent.* El Paso: Texas Western Press, 1991.

Kansas Historical Society. "Kansas Memory." Accessed July 12, 2011. www.kansasmemory.org.

Kroeger, Brooke. *Nellie Bly: Daredevil, Reporter, Feminist.* New York: Random House, 1994.

Peggy Hull Duell Collection. Kansas Collection, RH MS E66 (scrapbooks). Kenneth Spencer Research Library, University of Kansas Libraries, Lawrence, KS.

Peggy Hull Duell Collection. Kansas Collection, RH MS 130 (papers
and miscellaneous items, 1916–66), Boxes 1 and 2. Kenneth
Spencer Research Library, University of Kansas Libraries,
Lawrence, KS.

Osa Johnson

Adventure Lovers (Les amants de l'aventure). Directed by Michel
Viotte. May 2005. Released on DVD in the United States by
Washington, DC: National Geographic.

Johnson, Osa. *I Married Adventure: The Lives and Adventures of
Martin and Osa Johnson.* New York: Oxford University Press,
1997 (originally published 1940).

Martin and Osa Johnson Safari Museum, Archival Research Collection
and Permanent Exhibition, Chanute, KS.

Amelia Earhart

Earhart, Amelia. *The Fun of It: Random Records of My Own Flying and
of Women in Aviation.* New York: Brewer, Warren & Putnam, 1932.

Gillespie, Ric. *Finding Amelia: The True Story of the Earhart
Disappearance.* Annapolis, MD: Naval Institute Press, 2006.

Gillespie, Ric, in phone interview with the author, September 15,
2010.

Kansas Historical Society. "Kansas Memory." Accessed July 12, 2011.
www.kansasmemory.org.

INDEX

ABOUT THE AUTHOR

Gina Kaufmann is a freelance writer, storyteller, and broadcast journalist from Kansas City who dabbles in sheep farming and cheesemongering. She wrote a popular art column in the early 2000s and, more recently, co-hosted a daily public radio talk show alongside a local broadcast legend. In addition to the work she has done for local print and broadcast media, she has been involved in the New York–based *Heeb* magazine and its "Storytelling" series. Her essay, "Exquisite Suffering," will soon appear in the book *A Waiting Room of One's Own*. She has an MFA in creative writing from the University of British Columbia in Vancouver. Gina lives in a bungalow with her books, her boyfriend, and her herb garden—not necessarily listed in order of importance.